ILLUSTRATION WEST 34

A catalog of the 34th consecutive annual exhibition by
The Society of Illustrators of Los Angeles
held in the Japanese American Cultural & Community Center Gallery
Los Angeles, California

December 12th through December 23rd, 1995

REN WICKS

Ren Wicks has been a professional illustrator for over half a century. That in itself is amazing. The fact that he's still actively working and sees no reason to ever stop is astounding. While not old enough to be one of the founding fathers of this nation he was one of the founders of the Society of Illustrators of Los Angeles and of Group West, one of the finest collections of freelance illustrators on the West Coast.

He made his reputation as an artist who could make beer look better than it tasted and women look more beautiful than humanly possible. That second category has made him the venerated grand master at conventions dedicated to glamour. He painted for every major magazine back when that was the premier illustrative forum, has been noted for his minutely rendered aircraft, and has seen his artwork reproduced on billboards all across the country.

He's been President of the Society of Illustrators of Los Angeles on two occasions, has received its Lifetime Achievement Award, and he shows up, smartly dressed as always, at just about every Society event.

Ren has dedicated his life to illustration and to the Society of Illustrators of Los Angeles and it's with pleasure that we dedicate this Illustration West annual to him.

- Larry Salk, SILA Member, Lifetime Achievement Award Recipient

PRODUCED BY

Society of Illustrators of Los Angeles
116 The Plaza Pasadena
Pasadena, CA 91101 USA
Telephone: 818.551.1760
http: //www.Grafico.com/Grafico/sila/SilaHome.html

SCANS BY

Grafico Inc.
15320 Cornet Avenue
Santa Fe Springs, CA 90670
Telephone: 310.921.6731
           714.521.0620
Fax: 310.921.7038
www.GRAFICO.COM

PRINTED BY

Pacific Rim International Printing
11726 San Vicente Blvd.
Suite 280
Los Angeles, CA 90049
Telephone: 800.95 COLOR
           310.207.6336
Fax: 310.207.2566
http: //www.pacrim-intl.com

PRINTED IN HONG KONG

Illustration West 34
Society of Illustrators of Los Angeles

ISBN # 1-890466-00-X

TABLE OF CONTENTS

[SOCIETY OF ILLUSTRATORS OF LOS ANGELES]

BRIAR LEE MITCHELL

Early in my career, I learned that the greatest illustrators in the world were always willing to sit down and talk with me and share their expertise, tricks, tips and experiences. This demonstrated to me that they were working people with strength of character, enormous talent and heart. When you use this book, I hope that you can see the heart within these pages. This book is a compilation of the works selected from over 2,000 entries in the Illustration West Show 34. My thanks to the outstanding panel of judges who took upon themselves the enormous task of selecting those pieces you will see reproduced here.

A huge round of applause for Mr. Serge Michaels, the ILW34 Show Chair, who pulled a rabbit out of a hat by assembling the panel of judges and overseeing every phase of the show. None of this would be possible however, without the participation of the illustrators who entered the show and are sharing their work with you now. My personal thanks to all of you brave and hard working people.

One of the things that makes this such an outstanding compilation of work, is that the pieces which were accepted were judged by a panel of peers. This is not a book where the artist can buy a page such as in a source or trade book regardless of the quality of the work. It is important that you are aware of that.

My heartfelt thanks and congratulations to the medal winners, the juried entrants, our sponsors and to you, the owner of this book.

SERGE MICHAELS

I would like to take the time to say an enormous "Thank You" to all of the participating artists and hard working staff members who helped to make this great exhibit. History was made. This show garnered the most entries in SILA history. Congratulations!

This says something for the future of not only professional illustrators, but for SILA as well. For the past ten years, SILA has been working hard to make our mark not only on the West Coast, but expanding nationally as well. This work is paying off. Entries are higher than ever. Attendance at the shows and lectures are also high. This kind of momentum only serves to strengthen the industry as a whole. I wish SILA the best of luck and continued success in the future.

I'd like to also thank a few people who made the show such a fabulous success; to C.F. Payne for producing the most beautiful Call For Entries Poster art work, to Briter Concepts for their thoughtful vision in designing the CFE, to Grafico for their continued generosity in providing the outstanding color separations and to Comp-U-Artist for their exquisite attention to detail in printing our projects.

A mighty thanks to all of the judges whose enthusiasm and insightful vision chose the exquisite work you see on these pages. I also wish to acknowledge the hard work and support provided to me by the Board of Directors of SILA.

Enjoy!

DAVID BARTELS

David is perhaps the foremost visualist in advertising today. His hard hitting, memorable visuals have gained him world recognition and made him one of the most awarded art directors in the business. His posters have been featured on the Tonight Show. His advertising and design work has appeared in every major creative awards annual. Feature articles have been written about David in Print, American Showcase and Art Direction magazines. Three hard cover books on menus feature many of the menus David has designed. No wonder he is regularly called upon to judge the shows he has so often been represented in. With over 400 advertising and design awards to his credit, he has given J. Walter Thompson, N.W. Ayer, Campbell Mithun, Clinton E. Frank, and Leo Burnett good reason to be proud of their alumnus.

A few of David's clients include Allstate Insurance, Anheuser-Busch, Citizen Watch, General Mills, Icelandic Airlines, Kellogg's, Monsanto, Philip Morris and United Airlines.

THOMAS BLACKSHEAR

Thomas Blackshear went to work for Hallmark Card Company in Kansas City for one year after his 1977 graduation from the American Academy of Art in Chicago. While there he met illustrator, Mark English, and became his apprentice for several months. In 1980 he worked as head illustrator for Godbold/Richter Studio. He became a freelance illustrator in 1982, and has been self-employed ever since.

Known for his dramatic lighting and sensitivity to mood, Blackshear has produced illustrations for stamps, posters, plates, magazines, greeting cards, calendars, books and advertising. His clients include: Anheuser-Busch, Disney Pictures, Coca-Cola, Embassy Pictures, The Hamilton Group, International Wildlife, Jim Henson Studios, George Lucas Studios, Milton Bradley, National Geographic, Seven-Up, and Universal Studios.

For four consecutive years (1986-89), Blackshear illustrated a United States postal stamp for The Black Heritage Series, and in 1990 produced four 50th Anniversary Movie Poster stamps.

Twenty-eight of his depictions of famous Black Americans are represented in the 1992 Black Heritage Series. The Commemorative Book entitled *I Have a Dream*, and nineteen of the paintings are exhibited at the Smithsonian Institute in Washington, D.C. He also designed and executed illustrations for the Star Wars Collector Plates, the Wizard of Oz Movie Scene and Portrait Plates, the Star Trek Plates, and Star Trek, The Next Generation Plates. In addition, Thomas has created and sculpted a series of figurines for Hallmark, consisting of eight children-clowns called Innocent Wonders. He has taught at the San Francisco Academy of Art College, as well as lectured at numerous workshops throughout this country and in Sweden.

Blackshear's work has appeared in the Society of Illustrators Annuals 24, 25, 27, 28 and 30, and in the Outstanding American Illustrators Today Volume Two. He has received many awards, including: Gold and Silver Honors in the 1982 Kansas City Art Directors Club; two Gold Awards and Best-of-Show in 1986, Best-of-Show in 1989, and two Gold Awards in 1990 Illustrator West Shows; a Gold Medal in the 1988 National Society of Illustrators; two Silver Awards in the 1989 San Francisco Society of Illustrators Show; and the Plate of the Year Achievement Award in 1990.

Presently Blackshear is creating limited edition fine art prints for the Greenwich Workshop and limited edition Christian prints for the MasterPeace Collection of DaySpring.

In October, 1995, Blackshear and his wife, Ami, opened the Blackshear Gallery in Colorado Springs, Colorado.

Through Willits Designs, Blackshear has created a line of collectible figurines called Ebony Visions. He recently won the first runner-up for Artist of the Year and the Rising Star.

BRALDT BRALDS

Braldt Bralds is a self-taught illustrator who was working as a typographer in his native Holland in the 1960's. He answered a classified ad for a junior designer/illustrator with a Rotterdam advertising agency and soon was producing drawings for local newspapers. He recalls that those early drawings "really weren't very good."

Highly motivated, he kept drawing, and slowly his elegant style developed. "I learned my craft from the resources that were available, " he remembers. "Museums were a big influence. So were the Dutch masters, who produced such beautiful, precise work." He also studied the Illustrators Annual each year and was encouraged by such modern heavyweights as Wilson McLean and the late Richard Hess.

Braldt visited New York in 1978 as "the next logical step" in his career. A cover assignment for Time Magazine convinced him that the odds looked good for success in this country. So, in 1980, he moved to New York City with his wife and three cats.

A trickle of assignments grew to a steady stream. His work has been featured in major magazines such as Graphis, Idea Magazine (Japan),

MICHAEL DUDASH

As an artist and illustrator, C. Michael Dudash has always felt drawn to creating paintings that focus the viewer on the moment of beauty, empowered by a sense of atmosphere and spirit. In the last 16 years, he has learned to be successful at portraying these qualities in his hundreds of commissions; for publishers, design firms, corporations and advertising agencies. In the past years, Michael's oil paintings have won him a national reputation and numerous awards from the Society of Illustrators of Los Angeles and New York, the Society of Publication Designers, Communication Arts and How Magazine. He has written and published articles for American Artist, the Artists Magazine and Step-by-Step Graphics. He has featured his work as a guest lecturer at Washington University, St. Louis, Mo., the Rhode Island School of Design, the Society of Illustrators of Los Angeles, the Graphic Artist Guild in Vermont, the Kansas City Art Director's Club and taught an illustration class for the Vermont Community College.

Michael's clients include AT&T, Boca Raton Resort & Club, Clint Eastwood, Eddie Bauer, McGraw-Hill Publishing Co., MGM/United Artist, NBC, Paramount Pictures, Simon & Schuster, US Postal Service and the

member in the American Institute of Graphic Arts (AIGA), New York, The Society of Illustrators, New York, and Bookbuilders West, San Francisco.

He has interviewed on the campuses of the Art Center College of Design, Pasadena, California; The Art Academy, San Francisco, California; and The Rhode Island School of Design, Providence, Rhode Island. Michael established the Harcourt Brace annual scholarship for illustrators at Art Center, College of Design in Pasadena, California, now in its fifth year.

His book design and art direction have

been recognized for excellence by the American Institute of Graphic Arts, The American Library Association, Bookbuilders West, The Dimensional Illustrators Show, The Society of Illustrators, and Communication Arts and Print magazines.

ANN FIELD

Communication Arts, Novem Gebrauchsgrafik (Germany), and numerous Dutch publications. His work has received gold and silver medals in distinguished art director clubs throughout the United States. In addition to winning gold and silver awards from the Society of Illustrators in Los Angeles and New York, Braldt was also awarded the LA Society's Joseph Morgan Henninger Award for best of show and the NY Society's Hamilton King Award for best of show.

In 1993, Braldt was invited to serve on the International Advisory Board of the Art Institutes International. An illustration scholarship has been established in his name.

Some of his clients include Grand Marnier, The St. Louis Zoo and Texas Monthly Magazine.

United Nations among many others.

As a Christian, he is also highly focused on creating work to spread his belief in Jesus Christ and the Gospels. According to Michael, "The paintings attempt to be an inspiration and things of beauty themselves, but more importantly they hopefully trigger something greater in the viewer."

MICHAEL FARMER

After studying art and design at California College of Arts and Crafts in Oakland, California, and design and printing at California Polytechnic State University in San Luis Obispo, California, Michael Farmer has worked for the past 14 years in book publishing.

Currently Vice President, Director of Design and Production for the Trade Book Division, he oversees all creative and manufacturing aspects for over 300 adult and childrens' books published annually. In addition, he has held creative positions with the Harcourt Brace College and School textbook divisions. He is an active

Ann Field was educated at the Brighton College of Art, England (Bachelor of Honors Degree).

Her work experiences have included positions on the London Evening Standard as Fashion Writer, Art Director and Illustrator, and Fashion Editor for Mademoisselle and Italian Vogue. Ann also taught classes with the renowned Fashion Illustrator, Antonio Lopez.

Her clients include Warner Brothers Records, Harpers Bazaar, Bloomingdales, Barneys New York, Esprit, Swatch, Amfar, Estee Lauder, Starbucks and Madonna. Ann has also received numerous awards for her work, including Creativity Magazine (1984), Print Magazine "Design Excellence" (1988), Art Director's Club of Los Angeles (1990), Communication Arts (1992) and 3D Show New York City "Best in Show" (1996).

Permanent Installations and Murals include Barneys New York Apothecary, Quadrangle Grill, Dallas, Water Grill, Los Angeles, Harper Collins Reception, San Francisco and The Bungalow, Corona del mar, California.

MARY GRANDPRE'

Educated at the Minneapolis College of Art and Design, Mary GrandPre' began her career as a conceptual illustrator for local editorial clients.

Continually experimenting with media, Mary underwent many artistic changes in her expressive visual form. Her concerns for light, color, drawing and design came together in evocative, ethereal pastel paintings.

Mary's new work attracted corporate and advertising clients in addition to editorial. Some of her clients include. Ogilvy and Mather, BBD&O, Whittle Communications, The Richards Group, Neenah Paper, Atlantic Monthly Magazine, Random House, Berkley, Penguin, Deli and McGraw Hill publishers.

Mary's work has received national recognition through awards received from: the Society of Illustrators of Los Angeles and New York, Communication Arts, Graphis, Print, Art Direction and Diesi. Her work was chosen among thousands of illustrators to be on the cover of Showcase 16, and an article was written about her "concepting editorial assignments" in Step by Step Graphics.

Croton-on-Hudson. He has illustrated numerous children's books, magazine articles, record album covers, book jackets, advertising assignments, and is the designer of eleven commemorative stamps for the U.S. Postal Service.

He has received awards from the New York Society of Illustrators, A.I.G.A., book shows, art directors clubs across the country, and is the winner of the American Library Association-Coretta Scott King Award for 1986, 1987 and 1989. He has also won the Caldecott Honor Book Award for 1989, 1990 and 1995; 1990 Golden Kite Award, The Year's Best Illustrated Books for Children 1989 and 1995, The New York Times. He is concentrating on illustrating children's books and is published internationally.

In 1982 he was invited to serve on the U.S. Postal Service "Citizens Stamp Advisory Committee", and appointed to the Quality Assurance Committee in 1986. In 1982 he was invited to join the NASA Artist Team for the Space Shuttle Columbia.

Mr. Pinkney was visiting critic for the Rhode Island School of Design in 1969 and 1970, and Associate Professor for the Pratt Institute, Brooklyn, New York in 1986. He was Visiting Professor of Art at the University of Delaware, 1986 and 1988; Associate Professor of Art at the University of Delaware 1988-92; Professor of the Art Department of the University of Buffalo for 1991.

He has had one man shows in museums and galleries across the U.S. and group shows in Europe and Japan.

Mr. Pinkney has received the Alumni Award for 1992 from the Philadelphia College of Art and Design and has been honored for his work with a citation for Children's Literature from Drexel University and with the David McCord Children's Literature Citation

---

many of his favorite projects that used illustration.

More recently he has had less opportunity to work with illustrators, but has continued to do so whenever possible, e.g. with Drew Struzan on the "The Muppets Christmas Carol" and "The Muppets Treasure Island," with Morgan Weistling on "Homeward Bound II," and with Michael Dudash and David Grove on several projects.

David's own current computer imaging work owes a large debt to them, as well as to many other wonderful illustrators.

KENT WILLIAMS

Draftsman and painter, illustrator and comics creator, Kent Williams moved to New York in 1980 to study at the Pratt Institute where he received his BFA in Drawing and Painting. His graphic novel/comics work includes *Tell Me*, *Dark Meltdown* and *Blood: A Tale*.

A selection of his work on paper, *Kent Williams: Drawings & Monotypes* was published in 1991, and a catalogue of his paintings, *Kent Williams: Selected Works*, was published in 1995. His illustrations have been printed in numerous national and international publications, including Playboy,

Additionally, Mary has taught at the School of Associated Arts in St. Paul, Minnesota and she has also been a frequent guest lecturer at other fine schools.

JERRY PINKNEY

McCord Children's Literature Citation from Framingham State College. In 1996 he was the recipient of the 1996 Keen State College Children's Literature Festival Award.

DAVE RENERIC

national and international publications, including Playboy, Omni, and The Learning Channel Magazine.

Kent is the recipient of a number of awards for his work, both in comics and illustration. They include "The Yellow Kid"; Lucca, Italy's prestigious comics award, two medals from the Society of Illustrators, New York, and "The Joseph Henninger Award" for Best of Show from the Society of Illustrators of Los Angeles Illustration West 32.

Kent now lives in Chapel Hill, North

Carolina with his wife, Sherilyn, and their two sons, Kering and Ian.

Jerry Pinkney, born 1939, a native of Philadelphia, studied at the University of the Arts. In 1960 he moved to Boston, Massachusetts and began his career as an illustrator/designer for the Rustcraft Publishing Company. Upon leaving Rustcraft, he was employed by the Barker-Black Studio. Two years later, he and two other artists opened Kaleidoscope Studio. In 1968 he opened his own studio. This was the beginning of his career as a freelance artist.

In 1971 he moved to the New York area and opened Jerry Pinkney, Inc., operating out of his studio in

David Reneric is the Creative Director of Reneric and Company which specializes in print advertising for the motion picture industry. David became involved with illustration in the late seventies, working as an art director with Tony Seiniger.

Since 1978, he has had the opportunity to work with many of the best realistic illustrators in the country on campaigns for all of the major movie companies.

In the eighties, he, Jeffrey Bacon and Drew Struzan, produced the exhibition catalog *Dreams for Sale*, featuring

ILLUSTRATOR
BRAD HOLLAND

MEDIUM
OIL ON BOARD

ART DIRECTOR
JIM MC CLURE

CLIENT
MIND POWER

The illustration business has consistently experienced change...

In the past two decades the illustration business has changed in many ways. Opinions may vary, but most would say these changes have been negative and few positive. Some of the contributing factors that have shaped these points of view are the decline of the editorial market, growing numbers of good illustrators and the large amounts of photography and digital imagery being used.

One consistent opinion is that there are fewer venues with high visibility where illustration is used. This makes quality publications and juried annuals even more important. The growth of the SILA organization and their annual is a welcome contribution to the illustration industry on a national level. The SILA annual, if handled with the same integrity and enthusiasm as in the past, can only benefit the illustration business.

A smaller editorial market, more competition and the large amount of photography and digital images may well be the direction of the illustration business. This might be interpreted as negative although I feel that there are just as many positive aspects in today's illustration market. The increased amount of animation, multi-media, the large amount of work on the World Wide Web, video and the more obscured borders between art and illustration make a much more healthy climate than even that of twenty years ago. Who better to handle these broadened areas in the workplace than an illustrator who is fundamentally founded in image building, possesses great skill with media and can visually narrate with his or her own individuality.

John English

The illustration business has consistently experienced change with the advancement of technologies. There is no reason to think that it would not evolve into something different today or in the near future. I feel there are two ways to prepare yourself. First; simply be better than everybody else for there will always be a place for the very best. Second; look at what is going on now and what you believe will happen in the near future and follow your instincts. Change can be difficult and sometimes painful, but for those who are willing, they are the future.

SILA continues to offer opportunities for students...

Every year it seems that a smaller percentage of graduates nation-wide are choosing to freelance due to large student loan obligations. SILA awards scholarships to deserving national illustration students in the hope that the ever increasing financial burden of tuition expenses can be lessened, therefore allowing more students the opportunity to have more options available to them as professional artists. SILA continues to offer opportunities for students to meet and interact with their peers in addition to professionals in the field. SILA's educational seminars help to educate students about the business of illustration, promoting positive reinforcement regarding ethical business practices, offering pricing guidelines, and useful information about self-promotion. In addition to the seminars, guest speakers help to bridge the gap between being a student and what life is like working as a professional. This gives students an opportunity to meet and talk with professional illustrators they might admire. For national students, SILA provides a practical link to the professional world of commercial illustration.

Brad Weinman

On a more personal note, I became a SILA member when I was a student in my junior year. Immediately, I felt a sense of comradery. It was comforting to exchange stories of daily stress, lack of sleep, countless frustrations and triumphs; ultimately realizing that others had gone through similar trials while finding their own niche in this industry. I feel it's important, once you have established yourself, to give something back in whatever you feel comfortable. In this way future artists and current professionals can benefit from your experience and wisdom. A selfless contribution, no matter how large or small is the kind of thing that makes the world go around. Optimistically, I believe that this can only help to improve the illustration industry as a whole, including each person's personal journey we call life. The SILA student scholarship program continues to be a fulfilling aspect in my career, enabling me to help future illustrators make some sense of what the "real world" is like once you leave the comfortable nest of the school environment. It is inspiring to see students as well as professionals in illustration use this form of visual communication as a conduit for personal expression and greater meaning to their lives. I feel very fortunate to be able to pursue my passion in art, and make a living from it simultaneously. I still relate to what it is like to be a student, questioning what the future will hold for us as artists. I think the future looks bright for those that have the will and determination to see their goals realized.

I wish to thank all of the student scholarship sponsors, past and present, for not only giving back, but for investing in the future of illustration. One of the best pieces of advice ever given to me is "Do what you love, love what you do, and the rest will follow. "Be true to your heart."

Never believe compliments.

People like to call me an illustrator. I don't think of myself as only that, I like to call myself an Image Maker. Most Illustrators get work because the Art Directors have a preconceived idea of what they expect from the artist. However, the leaps I have made have to do with being allowed to just create something: whether it be photographic, line, painting or collage. I solve problems in different ways, *intuitively*. I don't look at life and see ugliness and destruction because that is not the truth. I see good, but not consciously, I guess I intuitively see good and that comes across in my work, whether it is a mark I make or a choice I make when selecting an item for a collage. It's funny, I am a serious person whose work doesn't look serious, yet the work is *real*. My passions in life amount to a list of two. TRUTH and BEAUTY. How do I go about finding those things? First, I'd like to quote from Coco Chanel: "Fashion is in the air. It is borne upon the wind. One intuits it. It is in the sky and on the macadam. It comes from ideas. Manners. Events". Watch, listen. Make a rule. Tell yourself, "It won't happen unless you really want it too. What do you understand well? What are your passions? What do you love? You have to be passionate about your work. It has to be like falling in love. The single most important thing in your life. OK?

Remember, in the middle of difficulty lies opportunity. The philosophy of Bruce Weber brings that home. When asked how he decides to work in color or black and white, he answers: "It depends on how you feel about what you are photographing. I was just recently photographing a young musician who is from Boston. He's in a heavy metal group and he's very pale, because musicians, unless they're from California or Hawaii, are always in the recording studio or on tour. I would normally have wanted to photograph him in color because he was so pale. It just depends on how you are seeing the photograph. You get up in the morning and you say, OK, I'm going to go out and take some photographs of this couple who are madly in love and it's gonna be really dramatic. They're so great looking together." Then you get out there and the light's really ugly, and they're having an argument instead of saying "Oh my God, I can't do the pictures,", wait a second, it's starting to rain, and the color is always so beautiful in the rain and maybe this story should be about them being separate not together. You've just got to be able to turn things around in your life all the time.'

Ann Field

Be a creator, not an observer. The artist should be in control. Nurture the things that other people let go of. Never believe compliments. It is not your business to question yourself or your work, how good it is or how smart it is, or how it compares to others. It is your business to keep it yours, clearly and directly to keep the channel open. The result is not satisfaction, but a queer, divine dissatisfaction which keeps us marching and makes us more alive! Be Brilliant!

There are too many bad books with good covers.

As an art director of books, I am bound to the written word. The best writing does not need to be illustrated. A well written book, for children or adults, provokes the imagination. It makes reading a book an intimate experience that asks the reader to respond to who they are, where they've been, what they know, what they've seen, and what they've read before. A book poorly written can never be salvaged by good, or even great illustration. A good actor can't save a bad play, no matter how capable their acting is, no matter how beautifully the set is designed.

I am fortunate to work for a publisher, Harcourt Brace & Company, whose reputation over the past 75 years is critically based on editorial integrity. Good writing is my means to good book design and illustration. When a well written book for children is illustrated with insight and inspiration, it complements the writing and adds dimension to the experience of reading. The best illustration does

not mirror the text, it expands it. Illustration in context to narrative story telling should be more a reaction than a reflection. I want an artist to show me what they individually "see" in a story, not a snapshot description of the text. I don't want someone to illustrate the obvious. It is redundant. Cinemagraphic technique is a wonderful model in visualizing text for illustration. Editing imagery is critical. Pacing is essential. Images are very dependent on their relationship to preceding the following images. The illustrator, like the film maker, has the freedom to orient the viewer to any perspective and point of view to achieve the desired impact. The intention of both mediums should be to connect the individual to the emotion of the story, to make them an active participant; not an observer apart from the story.

I'll confirm as an insider, you cannot judge a book by its cover. There are too many bad books with good covers. Publishers use book jackets primarily to function as marketing devices for their books. They are not intended to perform as narrative illustration to tell you what the book is about. Their intent is to arrest your attention and get you to stop and pick up the book. You will, hopefully, discover once the book is in your hands, what it is about and if it is worth purchasing. Good book jacket illustration is the most important advertising any publisher can do for a book. It is impulse oriented packaging.

Reviewers read the book to judge it, on its own, in advance forms without a jacket or cover; no marketing allowed. Consumers rely upon the opinions of reviewers, or their own impression of the book conveyed by its jacket or cover. The challenge for illustrators in this market is to make a compelling attempt to engage a potential reader with the piece of art, without gross misrepresentation of the content. Strength of concept is essential. Whatever the concept, when executed it must have impact. Impact isn't necessarily complex, loud, bold, bright and aggressive, although it could be. It could as easily be something simple, quiet, soft and subdued. Whatever voice the image has, in any manner, it should be distinctive and memorable.

Defining distinction isn't easy. I see it most often in illustrations with unpredictable and original concepts. Those are the illustrations in this year's show that impressed me, that I remember. Substance over style. There are plenty of technicians in the ranks of professional illustration. We need more thinkers.

INSTITUTIONAL

GOLD MEDAL

THOM ANG

SILVER MEDAL

GREGORY MANCHESS

BRONZE MEDAL

SERGE MICHAELS

ILLUSTRATOR
THOM ANG

MEDIUM
ACRYLIC, OIL, COLLAGE, PHOTOGRAPHY

ART DIRECTORS
LARRY DALLY, ELISABETH VINCENTELLI, JOAN HILTY

AGENCY
ALLEN SPIEGEL FINE ARTS

ILLUSTRATOR
JUI ISHIDA

MEDIUM
MIXED

ART DIRECTOR
STEVE HESS

CLIENT
HALLMARK CARDS

3

ILLUSTRATOR
JUI ISHIDA

MEDIUM
MIXED

ART DIRECTOR
STEVE HESS

CLIENT
HALLMARK CARDS

4

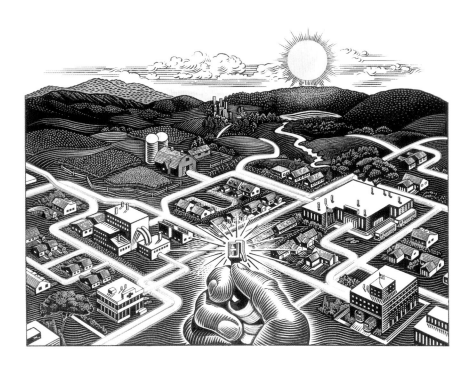

ILLUSTRATOR
ROGER XAVIER

MEDIUM
SCRATCHBOARD COPIED ONTO
WATERCOLOR PAPER

ART DIRECTOR
LEIGH BRINKLEY

AGENCY
BRINKLEY DESIGN

CLIENT
BELL SOUTH

5

ILLUSTRATOR
CHARLY PALMER

MEDIUM
ACRYLIC, MARBLEIZED PAPER

AGENCY
T. P. DESIGN

CLIENT
SOUTHERN BELL

6

ILLUSTRATOR
LISA FRENCH

MEDIUM
ACRYLIC

ART DIRECTOR
DIANE WOOLVERTON

CLIENT
US INFORMATION AGENCY

7

ILLUSTRATOR
FRANK STEINER

MEDIUM
OIL ON PAPER

ART DIRECTOR
MICHAEL TURNER

AGENCY
MARITZ INC.

CLIENT
BUICK

8

ILLUSTRATOR
ALAN MAZZETTI

MEDIUM
MIXED

CLIENT
NOBLEWORKS

9

ILLUSTRATOR
JACK MOLLOY

MEDIUM
COPPER ENGRAVING

ART DIRECTOR
SARAH BOLLES

CLIENT
CHRONICLE BOOKS

10

ILLUSTRATOR
BILL MAYER

CLIENT
GEORGIA PACIFIC PAPERS

11

ILLUSTRATOR
ROBERT M. CUNNINGHAM

MEDIUM
ACRYLIC ON PAPER

ART DIRECTOR
JENNIFER LAWSON

CLIENT
L. L. BEAN

12

ILLUSTRATOR
ROBERT M. CUNNINGHAM

MEDIUM
ACRYLIC ON PAPER

ART DIRECTOR
JENNIFER LAWSON

CLIENT
L. L. BEAN

13

ILLUSTRATOR
LINDA MONTGOMERY

MEDIUM
OIL ON CANVAS

ART DIRECTOR
MAXINE ROMBOUT

AGENCY
NOTES & QUERIES

CLIENT
PIERRE BELVEDERE INC.

14

ILLUSTRATOR
ROBERT M. CUNNINGHAM

MEDIUM
ACRYLIC ON MASONITE

ART DIRECTOR
JEFF TALBOT

AGENCY
GREENWICH WORKSHOP

CLIENT
US CANOE AND KAYAK TEAM

15

ILLUSTRATOR
MICHAEL ASTRACHAN

MEDIUM
AIRBRUSH, ACRYLIC

ART DIRECTOR
ELLIS ECHEVARRIA

CLIENT
THE MARLIN COMPANY

16

ILLUSTRATOR
LARRY MOORE

MEDIUM
PASTEL

ART DIRECTOR
MEREDITH RUSHING

AGENCY
RUSHING AND ASSOCIATES
DESIGN INC.

CLIENT
CENTRAL FLORIDA PRESS

17

ILLUSTRATOR
MARTHA ANNE BOOTH

CLIENT
FIRST IMPRESSIONS

18

ILLUSTRATOR
TED WRIGHT

MEDIUM
SILKSCREEN POSTER INKS

ART DIRECTOR
STEVE POLLACK

AGENCY
ARNOLD FORTUNA

CLIENT
NATIONAL BASEBALL LEAGUE

19

ILLUSTRATOR
DOUGLAS FRASER

MEDIUM
ALKYDS ON PAPER

ART DIRECTOR
ELANA FOUNDO

AGENCY
FP DESIGN INC.

CLIENT
NEW YORK UNIVERSITY

20

ILLUSTRATOR
LARRY MOORE

MEDIUM
PASTEL

ART DIRECTOR
JULIO LIMA

AGENCY
IT!

CLIENT
MAKE A WISH FOUNDATION

21

ILLUSTRATOR
DAVID HALEY

MEDIUM
CHALK PASTEL

ART DIRECTOR
JON PHILLIPS

AGENCY
MARITZ PERFORMANCE
IMPROVEMENT COMPANY

CLIENT
WASTE MANAGEMENT INC.

22

ILLUSTRATOR
DIRK WUNDERLICH

MEDIUM
AIRBRUSH ACRYLICS

ART DIRECTOR
DIRK WUNDERLICH

CLIENT
O. S. P. PUBLISHING

23

ILLUSTRATOR
BILL MAYER

CLIENT
GEORGIA PACIFIC PAPERS

24

ILLUSTRATOR
CHARLY PALMER

MEDIUM
ACRYLIC, MARBLEIZED PAPER

CLIENT
CITY OF MILWAUKEE

25

ILLUSTRATOR
BRAD HOLLAND

MEDIUM
ACRYLIC

ART DIRECTOR
MIKE SCRICCO

AGENCY
KEILER ADVERTISING

CLIENT
DELOITTE + TOUCHE

30

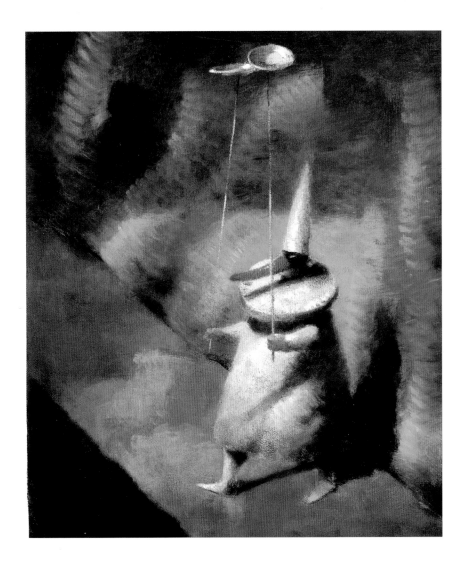

ILLUSTRATOR
BRAD HOLLAND

ART DIRECTOR
JANET LONGSTRETH

CLIENT
NEIMAN MARCUS

31

ILLUSTRATOR
GARY KELLEY

MEDIUM
PASTEL ON PAPER

ART DIRECTOR
DAVID BARTELS

AGENCY
BARTELS & COMPANY

CLIENT
ST. PATRICK'S CENTER

32

ILLUSTRATOR
BRAD WEINMAN

CLIENT
CAMBRIDGE TECHNOLOGIES
PARTNERS

33

ILLUSTRATOR
GARY KELLEY

MEDIUM
PASTEL ON PAPER

ART DIRECTOR
GARY KELLEY

CLIENT
SOHO JOURNAL, NEW YORK

34

ILLUSTRATOR
JIM DRYDEN

MEDIUM
ACRYLIC ON BOARD

ART DIRECTOR
MICHAEL TAYLOR

AGENCY
BIG DESIGN GROUP, LTD

CLIENT
COCA COLA

35

ILLUSTRATOR
BILL MAYER

CLIENT
GEORGIA PACIFIC PAPERS

36

ILLUSTRATOR
BILL MAYER

CLIENT
GEORGIA PACIFIC PAPERS

37

ILLUSTRATOR
ROBERT SPROUSE

MEDIUM
GOUACHE

ART DIRECTOR
LINDA LUNDSFORD/ LUNDSFORD
GRAPHICS

CLIENT
ILLUSTRATORS CLUB OF
WASHINGTON, DC, MD, VA

38

ILLUSTRATOR
THOM ANG

MEDIUM
ACRYLIC, OIL, COLLAGE,
PHOTOGRAPHY

ART DIRECTOR
GARY GERANI

AGENCY
ALLEN SPIEGEL FINE ARTS

CLIENT
THE TOPPS COMPANY

39

ILLUSTRATOR
THOM ANG

MEDIUM
ACRYLIC, OIL, COLLAGE,
PHOTOGRAPHY

ART DIRECTOR
GARY GERANI

AGENCY
ALLEN SPIEGEL FINE ARTS

CLIENT
THE TOPPS COMPANY

40

ILLUSTRATOR
DAVID BLOW

MEDIUM
DIGITAL, IRIS PRINT

ART DIRECTOR
DAVID BLOW

AGENCY
D B ADVERTISING

CLIENT
GRAFIK PRESS

41

ILLUSTRATOR
STEVEN RYDBERG

CLIENT
LORING CAFE, BAR AND
PLAYHOUSE

42

ILLUSTRATOR
THOM ANG

MEDIUM
ACRYLIC, OIL, COLLAGE,
PHOTOGRAPHY

ART DIRECTOR
GARY GERANI

AGENCY
ALLEN SPIEGEL FINE ARTS

CLIENT
THE TOPPS COMPANY

43

ILLUSTRATOR
JOHN ENGLISH

MEDIUM
OIL ON CANVAS

ART DIRECTOR
SHARYN O' MEARA

CLIENT
RAPHAEL HOTEL GROUP

44

ILLUSTRATOR
JOHN ENGLISH

MEDIUM
OIL ON CANVAS

ART DIRECTOR
SCOTT KIRKPATRICK

AGENCY
MILLER MEESTER ADVERTISING

CLIENT
PIONEER SEED COMPANY

46

ILLUSTRATOR
THOM ANG

MEDIUM
ACRYLIC, OIL, COLLAGE,
PHOTOGRAPHY

ART DIRECTOR
GARY GERANI

AGENCY
ALLEN SPIEGEL FINE ARTS

CLIENT
THE TOPPS COMPANY

47

ILLUSTRATOR
TED WRIGHT

MEDIUM
SILKSCREEN POSTER INKS

ART DIRECTOR
KEN LEVITAN

AGENCY
INTEGER GROUP

CLIENT
COORS

48

ILLUSTRATOR
JAMES GURNEY

CLIENT
GREENWICH WORKSHOP

49

ILLUSTRATOR
CLIFF NIELSEN

MEDIUM
DIGITAL

ART DIRECTOR
GARY GERANI, DON ALAN

CLIENT
TOPPS COMICS/ FOX

50

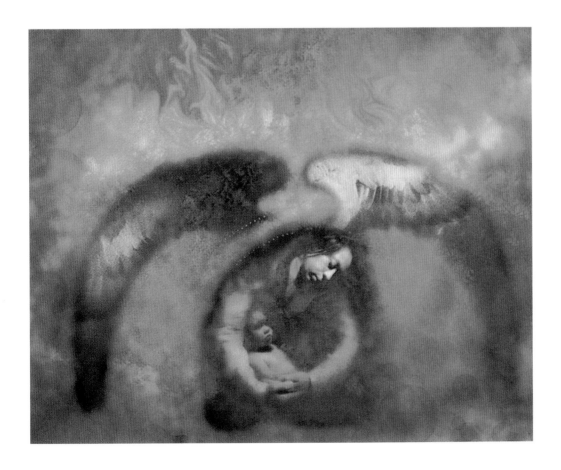

ILLUSTRATOR
CLIFF NIELSEN

MEDIUM
DIGITAL

ART DIRECTOR
GARY GERANI, DON ALAN

CLIENT
TOPPS COMICS/ FOX

5 I

ILLUSTRATOR
CLIFF NIELSEN

MEDIUM
DIGITAL

ART DIRECTOR
CLIFF NIELSEN, TERRI OWENS

AGENCY
STUDIO ZERO

CLIENT
WORLD VISION INTERNATIONAL

52

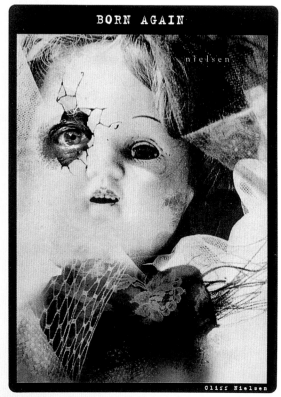

ILLUSTRATOR
CLIFF NIELSEN

MEDIUM
DIGITAL

ART DIRECTOR
CLIFF NIELSEN, TERRI OWENS

AGENCY
STUDIO ZERO

CLIENT
WORLD VISION INTERNATIONAL

53

INSTITUTIONAL

ILLUSTRATOR
KITTY MEEK

MEDIUM
OIL

ART DIRECTOR
MARC WARE

AGENCY
JOHN DOUGH ADVERTISING

CLIENT
DUNKIN DONUTS

54

ILLUSTRATOR
BRALDT BRALDS

CLIENT
GREENWICH WORKSHOP

55

ADVERTISING

GOLD MEDAL

ALBERT LORENZ

SILVER MEDAL

JOHN THOMPSON

BRONZE MEDAL

JOHN HOWARD

NOAH'S ARK

[ADVERTISING BRONZE MEDAL]

ILLUSTRATOR
JOHN HOWARD

MEDIUM
ACRYLIC ON CANVAS

ART DIRECTOR
TOM GROSSPIETSCH

AGENCY
TASSANI & PAGLIA

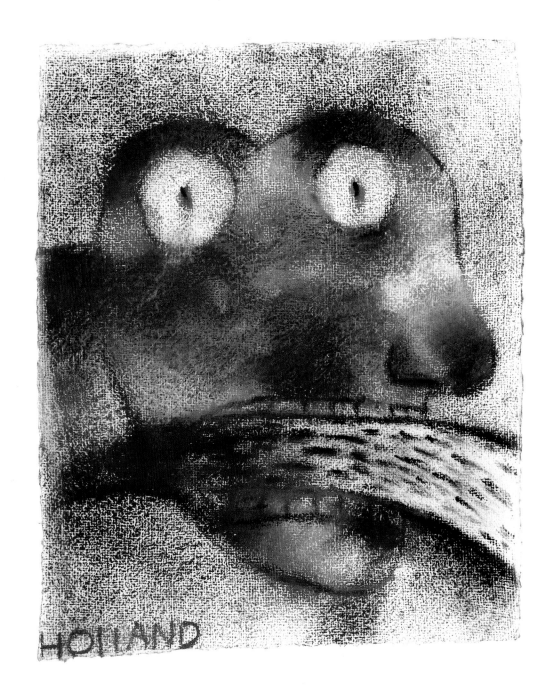

ILLUSTRATOR
BRAD HOLLAND

MEDIUM
PASTEL ON HANDMADE PAPER

ART DIRECTOR
JIM MC CUNE

CLIENT
CSCA

ILLUSTRATOR
MARTA RECIO

MEDIUM
ACRYLIC

ART DIRECTOR
BARBARA BETTIS

AGENCY
HAMAGAMI/CARROLL & ASSOCIATES

CLIENT
VIRGIN SOUND AND VISION/AMY SNELL

SALMON HOW YOU LIKE IT.

Gastronomy's salmon is flown in fresh on Delta Air Lines. ▲ *DELTA AIR LINES*

ILLUSTRATOR
DON WELLER

MEDIUM
COLORED PENCILS AND
OVERLAY FILM

ART DIRECTOR
DON WELLER

AGENCY
JOHN BECKER ADVERTISING

CLIENT
GASTRONOMY

61

ILLUSTRATOR
PAUL ROGERS

MEDIUM
ACRYLIC

ART DIRECTOR
SAL GARGUILLO

AGENCY

CLIENT
NAPPI ELRAN MURPHY

62

ILLUSTRATOR
EZRA TUCKER

MEDIUM
ACRYLIC

ART DIRECTOR
JORGE BALLARA

AGENCY
AYER CHICAGO

CLIENT
AYER CHICAGO

63

ILLUSTRATOR
TED WRIGHT

MEDIUM
SILKSCREEN POSTER INKS

ART DIRECTOR
WADE HOWELL

AGENCY
MARITZ INC.

CLIENT
NISSAN

64

ILLUSTRATOR
JOHN STEGER

MEDIUM
PASTEL

ART DIRECTOR
JOHN STEGER

AGENCY
MARITZ INC.

CLIENT
MICROAGE

65

ILLUSTRATOR
SUSAN GROSS

MEDIUM
INK

ART DIRECTOR
CAROL DAVIDSON AND
WHITNEY CRITCHLEY

AGENCY
NORDSTROMS

CLIENT
NORDSTROMS

66

ADVERTISING

ILLUSTRATOR
KAZUHIKO SANO

MEDIUM
ACRYLIC

ART DIRECTOR
DAVID GOLDEN

AGENCY
HAMILTON, CARVER & LEE

CLIENT
DUPONT PHARMACEUTICALS

69

ILLUSTRATOR
GREGORY MARTIN

MEDIUM
ACRYLIC

CLIENT
APPLIED MICRO CIRCUITS CORP.

70

ILLUSTRATOR
GUY PORFIRIO

MEDIUM
WATERCOLOR,
COLORED PENCIL

ART DIRECTOR
JOHN RAFFERTY

AGENCY
J. D'ADDARIO & COMPANY, INC.

CLIENT
J. D'ADDARIO & COMPANY, INC.

71

ILLUSTRATOR
GUY PORFIRIO

MEDIUM
MIXED

ART DIRECTOR
DAVID BELL

AGENCY
TRACY-LOCKE, DDB NEEDHAM

CLIENT
PEPSI-COLA

72

ILLUSTRATOR
KEN JOUDREY

MEDIUM
OIL

ART DIRECTOR
WARREN DOSSEY

AGENCY
PUBLIX SUPERMARKETS,
VISUAL MERCHANDISING DEPT.

CLIENT
PUBLIX SUPERMARKETS

73

ILLUSTRATOR
KEN JOUDREY

MEDIUM
OIL

ART DIRECTOR
BILL DAVIS

AGENCY
LISTER BUTLER INC.

CLIENT
TROPICANA

74

ILLUSTRATOR
KEN JOUDREY

MEDIUM
OIL

ART DIRECTOR
BILL DAVIS

AGENCY
LISTER BUTLER INC.

CLIENT
TROPICANA

75

ILLUSTRATOR
DOUGLAS FRASER

MEDIUM
DIGITAL
PHOTOGRAPHER: LEN DELESSIO

ART DIRECTOR
TORI WINN,
PALMA MC GOWAN

AGENCY
SONY STYLE

CLIENT
SONY

78

ILLUSTRATOR
DOUGLAS FRASER

MEDIUM
ALKYDS ON PAPER

ART DIRECTOR
MICHAEL HERNANDEZ

AGENCY
NIKE, INC.

CLIENT
NIKE

79

ILLUSTRATOR
PAM-ELA HARRELSON

MEDIUM
MIXED MEDIA

ART DIRECTOR
GORDY ROSS

AGENCY
SCOTT ARCHITECTURAL
GRAPHICS

CLIENT
THE YARMOUTH GROUP, INC.

80

ILLUSTRATOR
ALBERT LORENZ

MEDIUM
MULTI-MEDIA

ART DIRECTOR
RICHARD DEZINNO

CLIENT
BEPUZZLED

81

ILLUSTRATOR
ALBERT LORENZ

MEDIUM
MULTI-MEDIA

ART DIRECTOR
RICHARD DEZINNO

CLIENT
BEPUZZLED

82

ILLUSTRATOR
ALBERT LORENZ

CLIENT
BEPUZZLED

83

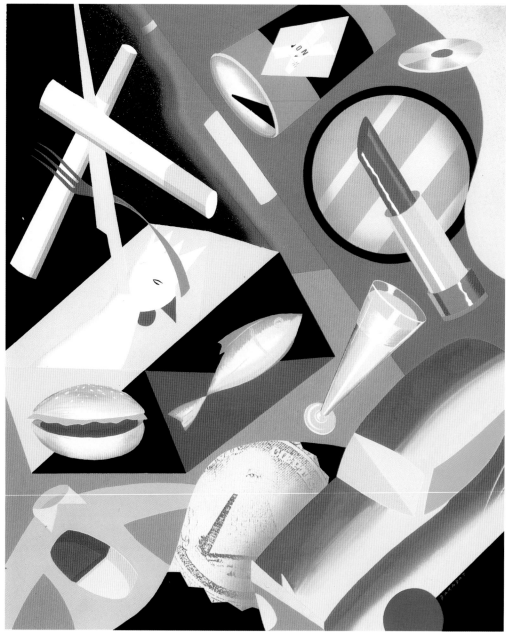

ILLUSTRATOR
GREGORY MANCHESS

MEDIUM
OIL

ART DIRECTOR
PATRICK HO

AGENCY
MS DESIGN GROUP

CLIENT
SAFEWAY STORES

88

ILLUSTRATOR
BRAD HOLLAND

MEDIUM
ACRYLIC ON MASONITE

ART DIRECTOR
GUY MARINO

AGENCY
DOREMUS & CO.

CLIENT
MICROSOFT

91

ILLUSTRATOR
BRAD HOLLAND

MEDIUM
OIL ON BOARD

ART DIRECTOR
JIM MC CLURE

CLIENT
MIND POWER

92

ILLUSTRATOR
BRAD HOLLAND

MEDIUM
ACRYLIC ON MASONITE

ART DIRECTOR
GUY MARINO

AGENCY
DOREMUS & CO.

CLIENT
BANKERS TRUST

93

ILLUSTRATOR
BRAD HOLLAND

MEDIUM
ACRYLIC ON MASONITE

ART DIRECTOR
ROBIN RAY

AGENCY
MAD DOG

CLIENT
SEATTLE REPERTORY THEATRE

94

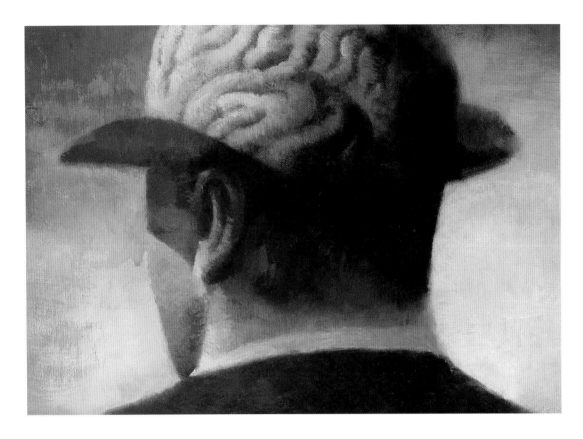

ILLUSTRATOR
BRAD HOLLAND

MEDIUM
OIL ON BOARD

ART DIRECTOR
JIM MC CLURE

CLIENT
MIND POWER

95

ILLUSTRATOR
BRAD HOLLAND

MEDIUM
OIL ON PASTEL

ART DIRECTOR
JIM MC CLURE

CLIENT
MIND POWER

96

ILLUSTRATOR
BRAD WEINMAN

MEDIUM
OIL ON PAPER

ART DIRECTOR
PAT BYRNES

AGENCY
DALIN SMITH & WHITE

CLIENT
SYBASE

99

ILLUSTRATOR
BILL MAYER

CLIENT
LEVI'S FOR WOMEN

100

ILLUSTRATOR
DOUGLAS TALALLA

MEDIUM
ACRYLIC

ART DIRECTOR
LORREN WATSON

AGENCY
DDB NEEDHAM

CLIENT
BROOKFIELD ZOO

101

ILLUSTRATOR
MARTA RECIO

MEDIUM
ACRYLIC

ART DIRECTOR
ERIC SMITH

AGENCY
HAMAGAMI/CARROLL &
ASSOCIATES

CLIENT
SEGA

102

ILLUSTRATOR
BILL MAYER

CLIENT
CREATIVITY

103

ILLUSTRATOR
JOHN ROWE

104

ILLUSTRATOR
SUSAN GROSS

MEDIUM
WATER COLOR & INK

ART DIRECTOR
MARK GUSTAFSTON

AGENCY
ANNE COCHRAN DESIGN

CLIENT
HERRERO CELLARS

105

EDITORIAL

GOLD MEDAL

BRAD HOLLAND

SILVER MEDAL

GREG SPALENKA

BRONZE MEDAL

GARY KELLEY

[EDITORIAL GOLD MEDAL]

ILLUSTRATOR
BRAD HOLLAND

MEDIUM
ACRYLIC ON MASONITE

ART DIRECTOR
DAVID CURCURRITO

CLIENT
PENTHOUSE

ILLUSTRATOR
GARY KELLEY

MEDIUM
PASTEL ON PAPER

ART DIRECTOR
FRED WOODWARD, GAIL ANDERSON

CLIENT
ROLLING STONE

[EDITORIAL HONORABLE MENTION]

ILLUSTRATOR
C.F. PAYNE

CLIENT
PENTHOUSE

109

ILLUSTRATOR

BILL CIGLIANO

MEDIUM

OIL AND GOUACHE

ART DIRECTOR

ROBERT MASON

CLIENT

LISTEN MAGAZINE

110

ILLUSTRATOR

DAVID BOWERS

MEDIUM

OIL ON MASONITE

ART DIRECTOR

DAVID WHITMORE

CLIENT

TLC MONTHLY

111

ILLUSTRATOR
ANTHONY FREDA

CLIENT
RAY GUN MAGAZINE

112

ILLUSTRATOR
DAVID O'KEEFE

MEDIUM
CLAY, MIXED MEDIA

ART DIRECTOR
PAT MITCHELL

CLIENT
TAMPA TRIBUNE

113

ILLUSTRATOR
ROBERT SHERRILL

MEDIUM
WATERCOLOR

ART DIRECTOR
FRED FEHLAU

CLIENT
PLAYBOY

114

ILLUSTRATOR
C.F. PAYNE

ART DIRECTOR
DAVID CURCURRITO

CLIENT
PENTHOUSE

115

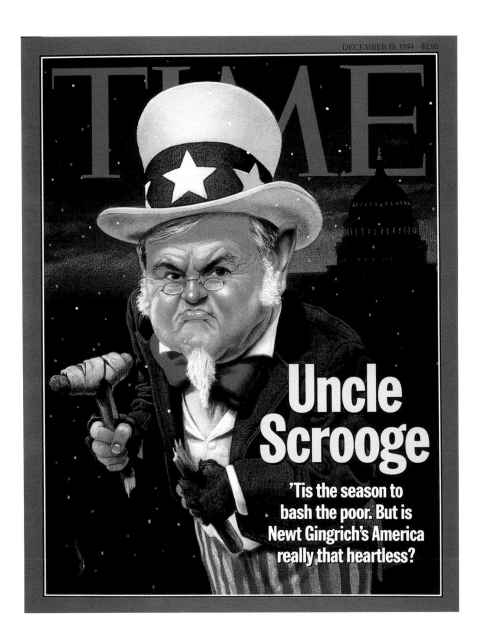

ILLUSTRATOR
C.F. PAYNE

MEDIUM
MIXED MEDIA

ART DIRECTOR
ARTHUR HOCHSTEIN

CLIENT
TIME MAGAZINE

116

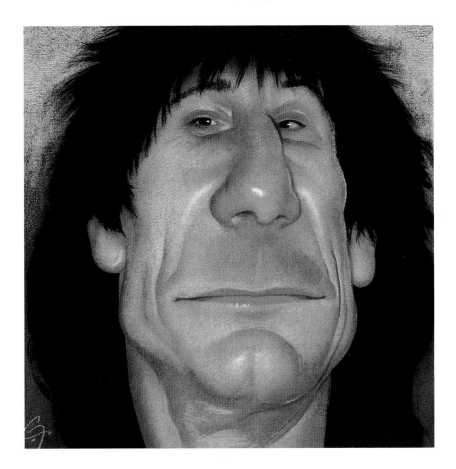

ILLUSTRATOR
C.F. PAYNE

MEDIUM
MIXED MEDIA

ART DIRECTOR
FRED WOODWARD

CLIENT
ROLLING STONE

117

ILLUSTRATOR

C.F. PAYNE

MEDIUM

MIXED MEDIA

ART DIRECTOR

STEPHEN HELLER

CLIENT

NEW YORK TIMES BOOK REVIEW

118

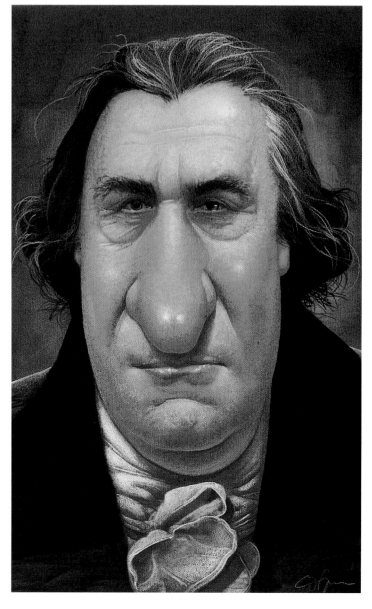

ILLUSTRATOR

DON ASMUSSEN

MEDIUM

PEN, INK, COLLAGE, AND DIGITAL

ART DIRECTOR

BILL GASPARD

CLIENT

SAN DIEGO UNION-TRIBUNE

119

ILLUSTRATOR
JIM MEYER

MEDIUM
MULTI-BLOCK WOODCUT

ART DIRECTOR
J. PORTER

CLIENT
YANKEE MAGAZINE

120

ILLUSTRATOR
LES KANTUREK

MEDIUM
LITHOGRAPH

ART DIRECTOR
WIL DONELLY

CLIENT
SMALL PRESS MAGAZINE

121

ILLUSTRATOR
TIM O'BRIEN

MEDIUM
OIL ON PANEL

ART DIRECTOR
KEN SMITH

CLIENT
TIME MAGAZINE, SPOTLIGHT PAGE

122

ILLUSTRATOR
KAZUHIKO SANO

MEDIUM
ACRYLIC

ART DIRECTOR
DAISUKE KOGA

AGENCY
SAURUS DESIGN

CLIENT
DINOSAUR FRONTLINE/GAKKEN

123

ILLUSTRATOR
TIM O'BRIEN

MEDIUM
OIL ON PANEL

ART DIRECTOR
MARY WORKMAN

CLIENT
ATLANTIC MONTHLY

124

ILLUSTRATOR
KAZUHIKO SANO

MEDIUM
ACRYLIC

ART DIRECTOR
DAISUKE KOGA

AGENCY
SAURUS DESIGN

CLIENT
DINOSAUR FRONTLINE/GAKKEN

125

ILLUSTRATOR

ADAM NIKLEWICZ

MEDIUM

ACRYLIC

ART DIRECTOR

JUDY GARLAND

AGENCY

ATLANTIC MONTHLY

CLIENT

ATLANTIC MONTHLY

126

ILLUSTRATOR

JULIETTE BORDA

MEDIUM

GOUACHE

ART DIRECTOR

EVA WOJNAR

CLIENT

AMERICAN AIRLINES

127

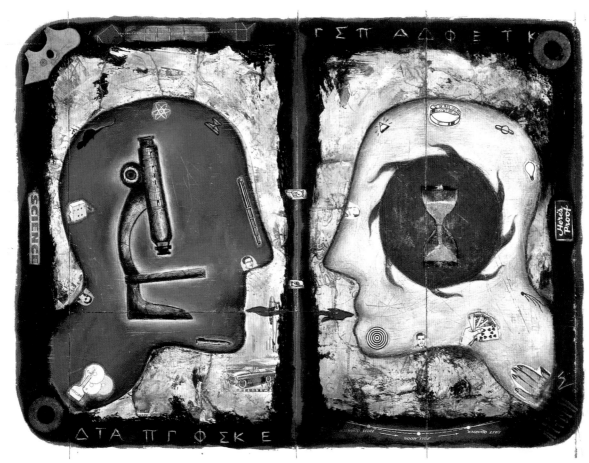

ILLUSTRATOR
SCOTT LAUMANN

MEDIUM
MIXED

ART DIRECTOR
CHRIS ROSS,
LAURIE HARKER

CLIENT
SAN DIEGO UNION-TRIBUNE

128

ILLUSTRATOR
HALSTEAD HANNAH

MEDIUM
SCRATCHBOARD,
WATERCOLOR

ART DIRECTOR
HULDA NELSON

CLIENT
SAN FRANCISCO CHRONICLE

129

ILLUSTRATOR

WILLIAM GEORGE

MEDIUM

OIL ON CANVAS

ART DIRECTOR

LORI FLEMMING

AGENCY

COWLES PUBLISHING

CLIENT

WILD WEST MAGAZINE

130

ILLUSTRATOR

JOHN H. HOWARD

MEDIUM

ACRYLIC ON CANVAS

ART DIRECTOR

ANDREA HEMMANN

AGENCY

HEMMANN DESIGN

CLIENT

SEVEN ARTS MAGAZINE

131

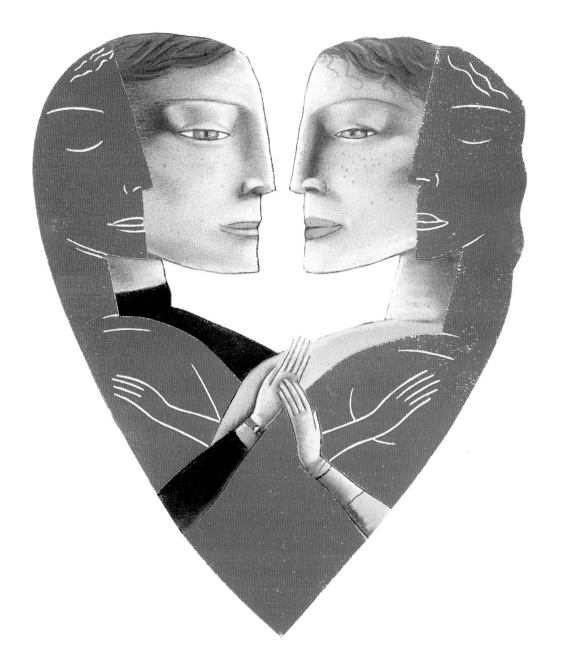

ILLUSTRATOR
WHITNEY SHERMAN

MEDIUM
PASTEL

ART DIRECTOR
EDNA JAMANDRE

CLIENT
THE BALTIMORE SUN

132

ILLUSTRATOR
GREGORY MANCHESS

MEDIUM
OIL

ART DIRECTOR
CHRIS SLOAN

CLIENT
NATIONAL GEOGRAPHIC
MAGAZINE

133

ILLUSTRATOR
BRAD HOLLAND

MEDIUM
ACRYLIC

ART DIRECTOR
WARREN CORBITT

CLIENT
GQ MAGAZINE

134

ILLUSTRATOR
BRAD HOLLAND

ART DIRECTOR
STEVE HELLER

CLIENT
NEW YORK TIMES

135

ILLUSTRATOR
BRAD HOLLAND

MEDIUM
ACRYLIC

ART DIRECTOR
JERRY PRICE

CLIENT
BREAKAWAY MAGAZINE

136

ILLUSTRATOR
BRAD HOLLAND

MEDIUM
ACRYLIC

ART DIRECTOR
D. J. STOUT

CLIENT
TEXAS MONTHLY

137

ILLUSTRATOR
GARY KELLEY

MEDIUM
PASTEL ON PAPER

ART DIRECTOR
FRED WOODWARD,
GAIL ANDERSON

CLIENT
ROLLING STONE

138

ILLUSTRATOR
GARY KELLEY

MEDIUM
PASTEL ON PAPER

ART DIRECTOR
LEANE BRENES NUCE

CLIENT
LOS ANGELES MAGAZINE

139

ILLUSTRATOR
GARY KELLEY

MEDIUM
PASTEL ON PAPER

ART DIRECTOR
CHRIS CURRY

CLIENT
NEW YORKER

140

ILLUSTRATOR
GARY KELLEY

MEDIUM
PASTEL ON PAPER

ART DIRECTOR
TOM STAEBLER,
KERIG POPE

CLIENT
PLAYBOY

141

ILLUSTRATOR
GREG SPALENKA

MEDIUM
MIXED

ART DIRECTOR
KERIG POPE

CLIENT
PLAYBOY

142

ILLUSTRATOR
BILL MAYER

CLIENT
OXFORD AMERICAN

143

ILLUSTRATOR
BILL MAYER

CLIENT
KIDSOFT MAGAZINE

144

ILLUSTRATOR
GREG SPALENKA

MEDIUM
MIXED

ART DIRECTOR
CHARLIE HESS

CLIENT
BUZZ

145

ILLUSTRATOR
JOHN S. DYKES

MEDIUM
WATERCOLOR, INK

ART DIRECTOR
JOAN MONTGOMERY

CLIENT
MAGAZINE WORKS

146

ILLUSTRATOR
JOHN S. DYKES

MEDIUM
MIXED

ART DIRECTOR
KENNETH B. SMITH

CLIENT
TIME MAGAZINE

147

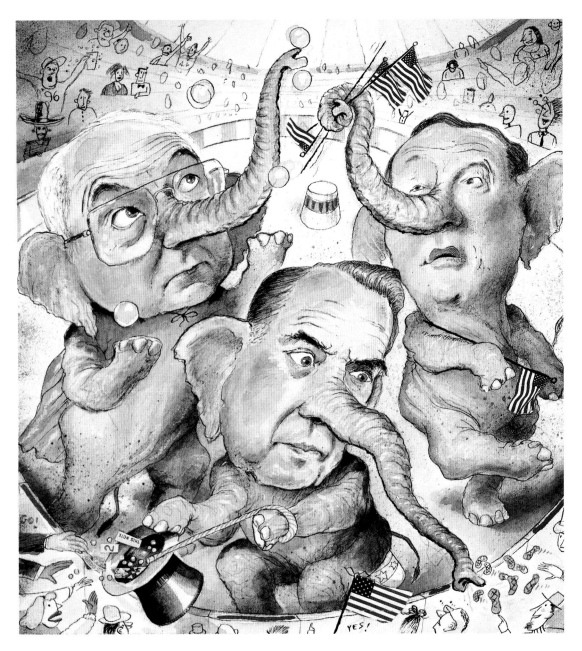

ILLUSTRATOR
JOHN S. DYKES

MEDIUM
WATERCOLOR, INKS, COLLAGE

ART DIRECTOR
PAUL LUSSIER

CLIENT
TIME MAGAZINE

148

ILLUSTRATOR

GREGORY MANCHESS

MEDIUM

OIL

ART DIRECTOR

DAVID WHITMORE

CLIENT

LEARNING CHANNEL MAGAZINE

149

ILLUSTRATOR

JOE SORREN

MEDIUM

ACRYLIC AND CRAYON ON
CANVAS

ART DIRECTOR

JOE MITCH,
JOE SORREN

CLIENT

TRANSWORLD SNOWBOARDING
MAGAZINE

150

ILLUSTRATOR
JOE SORREN

MEDIUM
ACRYLIC ON CANVAS

ART DIRECTOR
JONNY DONHOWE

CLIENT
WARP MAGAZINE

151

ILLUSTRATOR
JOE SORREN

MEDIUM
ACRYLIC ON CANVAS

ART DIRECTOR
JONNY DONHOWE

CLIENT
WARP MAGAZINE

152

ILLUSTRATOR

GARY TAXALI

MEDIUM

ALKYD ON MASONITE

ART DIRECTOR

DWAYNE FLINCHUM

CLIENT

INTELLICARD NEWS MAGAZINE

153

ILLUSTRATOR

RICK SEALOCK

MEDIUM

MIXED MEDIA/KITCHEN SINK

ART DIRECTOR

TOM FILLERBROWN

CLIENT

PULSE MAGAZINE

154

ILLUSTRATOR
FIAN ARROYO

MEDIUM
SCRATCHBOARD,
CEL-VINYL COLORS

ART DIRECTOR
ROBIN JOHNSTONE

AGENCY
CHICAGO TRIBUNE

CLIENT
CHICAGO TRIBUNE

155

ILLUSTRATOR
KARI KROLL

MEDIUM
COLLAGE, MIXED

ART DIRECTOR
CHRIS CURRY

CLIENT
THE NEW YORKER

156

ILLUSTRATOR
AMY NING

MEDIUM
AIRBRUSH

ART DIRECTOR
TIA LAI

CLIENT
THE ORANGE COUNTY REGISTER

157

ILLUSTRATOR
C. BRUCE MORSER

MEDIUM
PENCIL ON FILM

ART DIRECTOR
JESSIE NATHANS

CLIENT
SCIENTIFIC AMERICAN

158

ILLUSTRATOR
BRAD HOLLAND

MEDIUM
ACRYLIC ON MASONITE

ART DIRECTOR
SAM SHAHID

CLIENT
MIRABELLA

159

ILLUSTRATOR
BRAD HOLLAND

MEDIUM
ACRYLIC

ART DIRECTOR
KELLEY DOE

CLIENT
WASHINGTON POST

160

ILLUSTRATOR
JOHN ENGLISH

MEDIUM
OIL ON CANVAS

ART DIRECTOR
SUZANNE MORIN

CLIENT
AUDUBON MAGAZINE

161

ILLUSTRATOR
JORDAN ISIP

MEDIUM
MIXED

ART DIRECTOR
PATRICIA COUSINS

AGENCY
PATRICIA COUSINS

CLIENT
NORTHEAST MAGAZINE,
HARTFORD COURANT

162

ILLUSTRATOR
JORDAN ISIP

MEDIUM
MIXED

ART DIRECTOR
PATRICIA J. B. FLYNN

CLIENT
THE PROGRESSIVE

163

ILLUSTRATOR
JORDAN ISIP

MEDIUM
MIXED

ART DIRECTOR
ROBERT PRIEST

AGENCY
WARREN CORBITT

CLIENT
GQ MAGAZINE

164

ILLUSTRATOR
BRAD HOLLAND

MEDIUM
ACRYLIC ON MASONITE

ART DIRECTOR
NANCY HARRIS

CLIENT
NEW YORK TIMES MAGAZINE

167

ILLUSTRATOR
BRAD HOLLAND

ART DIRECTOR
STEVE HELLER

CLIENT
NEW YORK TIMES BOOK REVIEW

168

BOOK

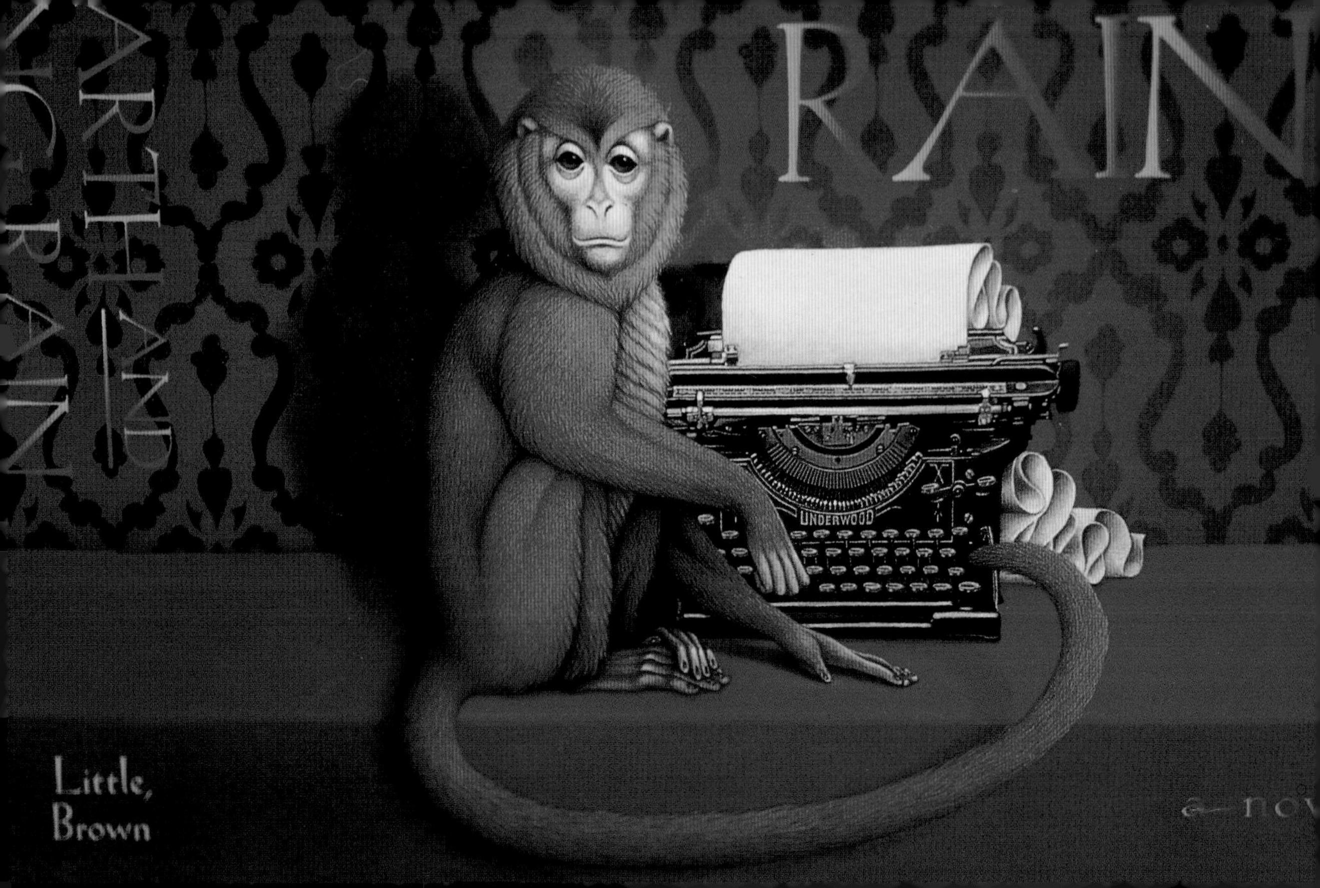
RAIN
UNDERWOOD
Little,
Brown

[BOOK SILVER MEDAL]

ILLUSTRATOR
WENDELL MINOR

MEDIUM
WATERCOLOR ON COLD PRESS BOARD

ART DIRECTOR
VAUGHN ANDREWS

CLIENT
HARCOURT BRACE & COMPANY

ILLUSTRATOR
TED RAND

MEDIUM
ACRYLIC ON GESSO

ART DIRECTOR
MICHAEL FARMER

CLIENT
HARCOURT BRACE

172

ILLUSTRATOR
JAMES GURNEY

CLIENT
TURNER PUBLISHING, INC.

173

ILLUSTRATOR
BRAD WEINMAN

MEDIUM
OIL ON PAPER

ART DIRECTOR
MICHAEL FARMER

CLIENT
HARCOURT BRACE & COMPANY

174

ILLUSTRATOR
JOHN THOMPSON

MEDIUM
ACRYLIC

ART DIRECTOR
CLAIRE COUNIHAN

CLIENT
SCHOLASTIC, INC.

175

ILLUSTRATOR
STEVE JOHNSON,
LOU FANCHER

MEDIUM
ACRYLIC ON PAPER

ART DIRECTOR
LOU FANCHER

CLIENT
VIKING/PENGUIN

176

ILLUSTRATOR
DAVE MC KEAN

MEDIUM
MIXED

ART DIRECTOR
DAVE MC KEAN

AGENCY
ALLEN SPIEGEL
FINE ARTS

CLIENT
DC COMICS/VERTIGO

177

ILLUSTRATOR
GARY KELLEY

MEDIUM
PASTEL ON PAPER

ART DIRECTOR
SUZANNE NOLI

CLIENT
HARPER COLLINS

178

ILLUSTRATOR
WENDELL MINOR

MEDIUM
ACRYLIC ON WOOD

ART DIRECTOR
FRANK METZ

CLIENT
SIMON & SCHUSTER

179

ILLUSTRATOR
CATHLEEN TOELKE

CLIENT
ATHENAEUM/MACMILLAN

180

ILLUSTRATOR
WENDELL MINOR

MEDIUM
ACRYLIC ON MASONITE PANEL

ART DIRECTOR
VAUGHN ANDREWS

CLIENT
HARCOURT BRACE & COMPANY

183

ILLUSTRATOR
WENDELL MINOR

MEDIUM
ACRYLIC ON MASONITE PANEL

ART DIRECTOR
VAUGHN ANDREWS

CLIENT
HARCOURT BRACE & COMPANY

184

ILLUSTRATOR
DAVID BOWERS

MEDIUM
OIL ON MASONITE

ART DIRECTOR
JAMES WANG

CLIENT
ST. MARTIN'S PRESS

185

ILLUSTRATOR
TIM O'BRIEN

MEDIUM
OIL ON PANEL

ART DIRECTOR
ELIZABETH PARISI

CLIENT
SCHOLASTIC

186

ILLUSTRATOR

JOEL PAROD

MEDIUM

OIL

ART DIRECTOR

ALAN DINGMAN

CLIENT

ST. MARTIN'S PRESS

187

BLACK & WHITE

BRONZE MEDAL

ROBERT MEGNACK

ENTERTAINMENT

GOLD MEDAL

ROBERT RODRIGUEZ

SILVER MEDAL

KINUKO CRAFT

BRONZE MEDAL

GARY KELLEY

♥

[ENTERTAINMENT GOLD MEDAL]

ILLUSTRATOR
ROBERT RODRIGUEZ

CLIENT
N.A.R.A.S.

[ENTERTAINMENT SILVER MEDAL]

ILLUSTRATOR
KINUKO CRAFT

MEDIUM
OIL, WATERCOLOR ON ILLUSTRATION BOARD

ART DIRECTOR
COLLENE CURRIE, DALLAS OPERA, CLAY FREEMAN, MAY & COMPANY

CLIENT
DALLAS OPERA

191

[ENTERTAINMENT BRONZE MEDAL]

[HONORABLE MENTION]

ILLUSTRATOR
GARY KELLEY

MEDIUM
PASTEL ON PAPER

ART DIRECTOR
GEORGE CORNELL

CLIENT
PENGUIN BOOKS

193

ILLUSTRATOR
GARY KELLEY

MEDIUM
PASTEL ON PAPER

ART DIRECTOR
GEORGE CORNELL

CLIENT
PENGUIN BOOKS

194

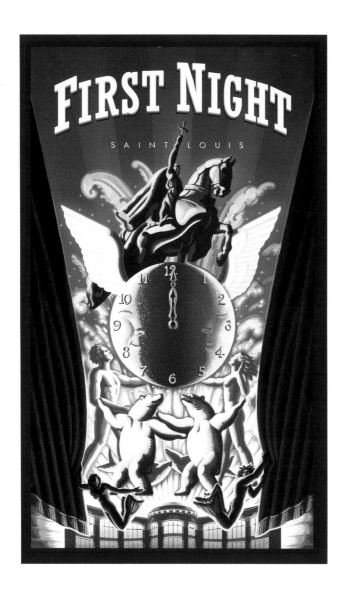

ILLUSTRATOR
BRYAN HAYNES

MEDIUM
ACRYLIC

ART DIRECTOR
PAM BLISS

AGENCY
KIKU OBATA & CO.

CLIENT
CITY OF ST. LOUIS

195

ILLUSTRATOR
MORGAN WEISTLING

MEDIUM
OIL

ART DIRECTOR
DAVID RENERIC

AGENCY
RENERIC & ASSOCIATES

CLIENT
DISNEY

196

ILLUSTRATOR
BRAD WEINMAN

MEDIUM
OIL ON PAPER

ART DIRECTOR
RIKKI POULOS

CLIENT
NATIONAL ACADEMY OF
RECORDING ARTS & SCIENCE

197

ILLUSTRATOR
DAVID BLOW

MEDIUM
DIGITAL, IRIS PRINT

ART DIRECTOR
DAVID BLOW

AGENCY
D B ADVERTISING

CLIENT
UNIVERSITY OF NORTH TEXAS
MUSIC DEPT.

198

ILLUSTRATOR
JOHN ENGLISH

MEDIUM
OIL ON CANVAS

ART DIRECTOR
RISA ZAITSCHECK

CLIENT
SONY MUSIC

199

ILLUSTRATOR
EZRA TUCKER

MEDIUM
ACRYLIC

ART DIRECTOR
SCOTT JOHNSON

AGENCY
BMG MUSIC

CLIENT
BMG CLASSICS

200

ILLUSTRATOR
MARIA STROSTER

MEDIUM
ACRYLIC ON BOARD

ART DIRECTOR
PATRICK PENNEY

AGENCY
R & B ENTERPRISES

CLIENT
THE STAGEBILL GROUP

201

ILLUSTRATOR
MICHAEL SCHWAB

MEDIUM
SCREEN PRINTED POSTER

ART DIRECTOR
BILL MERRIKEN

AGENCY
MICHAEL SCHWAB STUDIO

CLIENT
PERKIN SHEARER, CHILDRENS
HOME OF MINNESOTA

202

ILLUSTRATOR
KEITH PUCCINELLI

MEDIUM
DIGITAL, QUARK XPRESS

ART DIRECTOR
KEITH PUCCINELLI

AGENCY
PUCCINELLI DESIGN

CLIENT
SUMMER SOLSTICE
CELEBRATION

203

ILLUSTRATOR
ROBERT RODRIGUEZ

CLIENT
SONY RECORDS

204

ILLUSTRATOR
NORA KOERBER

MEDIUM
ACRYLIC

ART DIRECTOR
RIKKI POULOS

AGENCY
RIKKI POULOS DESIGN

CLIENT
N.A.R.A.S.

205

ILLUSTRATOR
JOEL NAKAMURA

MEDIUM
MIXED MEDIA ON TIN

ART DIRECTOR
SONY MEDIA

CLIENT
GRP RECORDS

206

ILLUSTRATOR
ADAM NIKLEWICZ

MEDIUM
ACRYLIC

ART DIRECTOR
JAN OHYE,
SALVATORE GARGIULLO

AGENCY
NAPPI, ELIRAN, MURPHY

CLIENT
NEW YORK CITY OPERA

207

ILLUSTRATOR
ADAM NIKLEWICZ

MEDIUM
ACRYLIC

ART DIRECTOR
DIANNE WOOLVERTON

CLIENT
UNITED STATES
INFORMATION AGENCY

208

ILLUSTRATOR
ADAM NIKLEWICZ

MEDIUM
ACRYLIC

ART DIRECTOR
JAN OHYE,
SALVATORE GARGIULLO

AGENCY
JAPPI, ELIRAN, MURPHY

CLIENT
NEW YORK CITY OPERA

209

ILLUSTRATOR
STEVE MILLER

CLIENT
N.A.R.A.S.

210

ILLUSTRATOR
MELINDA BECK

MEDIUM
MIXED

ART DIRECTOR
SATORU IGARASHI

CLIENT
ISLAND RECORDS

211

ILLUSTRATOR
PHIL BOATWRIGHT

CLIENT
20TH CENTURY FOX

212

ILLUSTRATOR
BRUCE GARRITY

MEDIUM
ACRYLIC

ART DIRECTOR
HEATHER YELLE

AGENCY
PARALLEL DESIGN INC.

CLIENT
APPEL FARMS ART & MUSIC
CENTER

213

ILLUSTRATOR
BRAD WEINMAN

MEDIUM
OIL ON PAPER

ART DIRECTOR
FRED FEHLAU

CLIENT
PLAYBOY

214

ILLUSTRATOR
BOB CONGE

MEDIUM
STEEL PEN, INK LINE, WATER
COLOR

ART DIRECTOR
LUANNE GRAFFEO

CLIENT
EM RECORDS

215

ILLUSTRATOR
BILL MAYER

CLIENT
CLEVELAND FILM FESTIVAL

216

SELF-PROMOTIONAL/ UNPUBLISHED

GOLD MEDAL

MARK ENGLISH

SILVER MEDAL

MARK ENGLISH

BRONZE MEDAL

HERMAN WEBB

ILLUSTRATOR

MARK ENGLISH

[SELF-PROMOTIONAL/UNPUBLISHED BRONZE MEDAL]

ILLUSTRATOR
HERMAN WEBB

CLIENT
OBLIQUE COMMUNICATIONS

[SELF-PROMOTIONAL/UNPUBLISHED HONORABLE MENTION]

ILLUSTRATOR
EZRA TUCKER

MEDIUM
ACRYLIC

ART DIRECTOR
EZRA TUCKER

220

[SELF-PROMOTIONAL/UNPUBLISHED HONORABLE MENTION]

ILLUSTRATOR
BILL MAYER

221

ILLUSTRATOR
PAUL R. ALEXANDER

MEDIUM
GOUACHE

222

ILLUSTRATOR
ERIC BOWMAN

MEDIUM
ACRYLIC ON STRATHMORE
BRISTOL

ART DIRECTOR
ERIC BOWMAN

223

**SELF– PROMOTIONAL
UNPUBLISHED**

ILLUSTRATOR
ERIC BOWMAN

MEDIUM
ACRYLIC ON BOARD

ART DIRECTOR
ERIC BOWMAN

224

ILLUSTRATOR
ERIC BOWMAN

MEDIUM
ACRYLIC ON BOARD

ART DIRECTOR
ERIC BOWMAN

225

**SELF- PROMOTIONAL
UNPUBLISHED**

ILLUSTRATOR
DAVID DOUGLASS

MEDIUM
OIL, COLORED PENCIL,
GRAPHITE

226

ILLUSTRATOR
MORGAN WEISTLING

MEDIUM
OIL

227

**SELF- PROMOTIONAL
UNPUBLISHED**

ILLUSTRATOR
DAVID WILLARDSON

228

ILLUSTRATOR
DAVID WILLARDSON

229

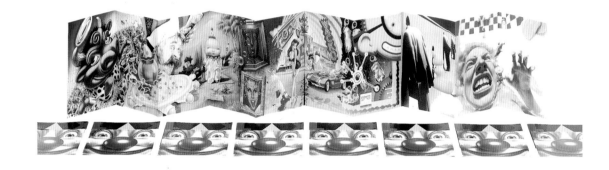

ILLUSTRATOR
BOB COMMANDER

230

SELF- PROMOTIONAL
UNPUBLISHED

ILLUSTRATOR
WAYNE GALLIPOLI

MEDIUM
OIL ON MASONITE

CLIENT
BURN/ WAYNE GALLIPOLI

231

ILLUSTRATOR
VALERIE J. HEGARTY

MEDIUM
ACRYLIC ON WOOD

232

ILLUSTRATOR
DANIEL MATHER

MEDIUM
ACRYLIC

233

ILLUSTRATOR
DANIEL MATHER

MEDIUM
ACRYLIC

234

**SELF– PROMOTIONAL
UNPUBLISHED**

ILLUSTRATOR
ALLAN BURCH

MEDIUM
ACRYLIC ON ILLUSTRATION
BOARD

ART DIRECTOR
ALLAN BURCH

235

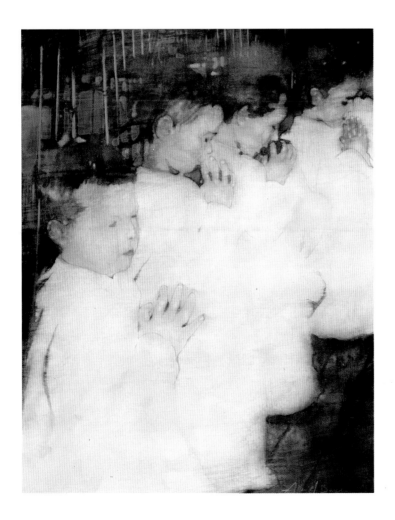

ILLUSTRATOR
ALLAN BURCH

MEDIUM
ACRYLIC ON ILLUSTRATION
BOARD

ART DIRECTOR
ALLAN BURCH

236

**SELF– PROMOTIONAL
UNPUBLISHED**

ILLUSTRATOR
ALLAN BURCH

MEDIUM
ACRYLIC ON ILLUSTRATION
BOARD

ART DIRECTOR
ALLAN BURCH

240

ILLUSTRATOR
MARK GARRO

MEDIUM
ACRYLIC ON CANVAS

ART DIRECTOR
MARK GARRO

CLIENT
SUBLIME DESIGN

241

SELF– PROMOTIONAL
UNPUBLISHED

ILLUSTRATOR
MARK GARRO

MEDIUM
ACRYLIC ON BOARD

ART DIRECTOR
MARK GARRO

CLIENT
SUBLIME DESIGN

239

ILLUSTRATOR
ALEX MURAWSKI

MEDIUM
ACRYLIC, INK ON ACETATE

ART DIRECTOR
DAVID WILLARDSON

AGENCY
WILLARDSON ASSOC.

CLIENT
LAX MAGAZINE

240

**SELF- PROMOTIONAL
UNPUBLISHED**

ILLUSTRATOR
BUKET ERDOGAN

MEDIUM
ACRYLIC ON CANVAS

241

ILLUSTRATOR
BUKET ERDOGAN

MEDIUM
ACRYLIC ON CANVAS

242

SELF- PROMOTIONAL
UNPUBLISHED

ILLUSTRATOR
DAVID BOWERS

MEDIUM
OIL ON MASONITE

243

ILLUSTRATOR
KYLE STONE

MEDIUM
ACRYLIC & GOUACHE

ART DIRECTOR
KYLE STONE

244

**SELF- PROMOTIONAL
UNPUBLISHED**

ILLUSTRATOR
EZRA TUCKER

MEDIUM
ACRYLIC

245

ILLUSTRATOR
DAVE MC KEAN

MEDIUM
MIXED

ART DIRECTOR
DAVE MC KEAN

AGENCY
ALLEN SPIEGEL FIN ARTS

CLIENT
FOUR COLOR IMAGES

246

SELF– PROMOTIONAL
UNPUBLISHED

ILLUSTRATOR
SCOTT MEDLOCK

MEDIUM
OIL

247

ILLUSTRATOR
YOUNG MO YOON

MEDIUM
COMPUTER

248

**SELF– PROMOTIONAL
UNPUBLISHED**

ILLUSTRATOR
PHILIP BLISS

MEDIUM
ACRYLIC

ART DIRECTOR
PHILIP BLISS

249

ILLUSTRATOR
DOUGLAS C. KLAUBA

MEDIUM
ACRYLIC AND PENCIL ON
ILLUSTRATION BOARD

250

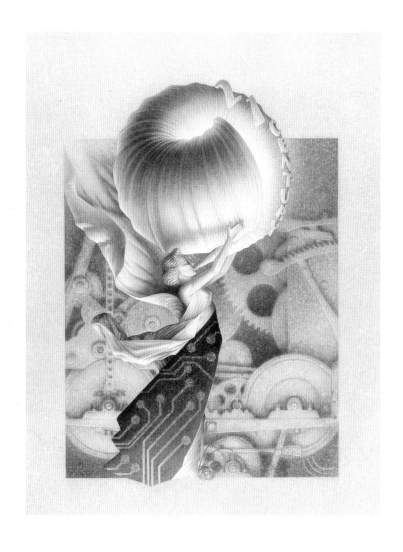

SELF- PROMOTIONAL
UNPUBLISHED

ILLUSTRATOR
DOUGLAS C. KLAUBA

MEDIUM
MIXED MEDIA

251

ILLUSTRATOR
SHELLY SHINJO

MEDIUM
ACRYLIC

252

**SELF– PROMOTIONAL
UNPUBLISHED**

ILLUSTRATOR
GREG TUCKER

MEDIUM
PASTEL

ART DIRECTOR
GREG TUCKER

CLIENT
CAROL CHISLOVSKY

255

ILLUSTRATOR
GREG TUCKER

MEDIUM
PASTEL

ART DIRECTOR
GREG TUCKER

CLIENT
CAROL CHISLOVSKY

256

**SELF- PROMOTIONAL
UNPUBLISHED**

ILLUSTRATOR
ELDON DOTY

MEDIUM
COMPUTER GENERATED

257

ILLUSTRATOR
ELDON DOTY

MEDIUM
COMPUTER GENERATED

258

SELF- PROMOTIONAL
UNPUBLISHED

ILLUSTRATOR
JIM PAILLOT

259

ILLUSTRATOR
DON ASMUSSEN

MEDIUM
PEN, INK, COLLAGE, AND DIGITAL

260

ILLUSTRATOR
DON ASMUSSEN

MEDIUM
PEN, INK, COLLAGE, AND DIGITAL

261

ILLUSTRATOR
DON ASMUSSEN

MEDIUM
PEN, INK, COLLAGE, AND DIGITAL

262

ILLUSTRATOR
MICHAEL WOLOSCHINOW

263

ILLUSTRATOR
ZHAOMING WU

264

ILLUSTRATOR
MARK COVELL

MEDIUM
OIL

ART DIRECTOR
MARK COVELL

265

ILLUSTRATOR
MARK COVELL

MEDIUM
OIL

266

SELF- PROMOTIONAL
UNPUBLISHED

ILLUSTRATOR
LES KANTUREK

MEDIUM
LINOLEUM-CUT

267

ILLUSTRATOR
MARTIN FRENCH

MEDIUM
DIGITAL

ART DIRECTOR
MARTIN FRENCH

CLIENT
PAT HACKETT ARTIST'S REP

268

ILLUSTRATOR
MARTIN FRENCH

MEDIUM
DIGITAL

ART DIRECTOR
MARTIN FRENCH

CLIENT
PAT HACKETT ARTIST'S REP

269

ILLUSTRATOR
MICHAEL SCHWAB

MEDIUM
SCREEN PRINTED POSTER

ART DIRECTOR
KEN SLAZYC

CLIENT
ART DIRECTOR'S CLUB OF
CINCINNATI

270

SELF- PROMOTIONAL
UNPUBLISHED

ILLUSTRATOR
GREGORY S. MARTIN

MEDIUM
OIL ON PANEL

271

ILLUSTRATOR
BRENT WATKINSON

MEDIUM
DIGITAL MIXED MEDIA

ART DIRECTOR
BRENT WATKINSON

272

SELF– PROMOTIONAL
UNPUBLISHED

ILLUSTRATOR
BRENT WATKINSON

MEDIUM
MIXED MEDIA

ART DIRECTOR
BRENT WATKINSON

273

ILLUSTRATOR
STEPHEN MAGSIG

MEDIUM
OIL/LINEN

274

SELF- PROMOTIONAL
UNPUBLISHED

ILLUSTRATOR
DONATO GIANCOLA

MEDIUM
OIL ON BOARD

275

ILLUSTRATOR
HEATHER ELMER

MEDIUM
WATER COLOR

276

**SELF– PROMOTIONAL
UNPUBLISHED**

ILLUSTRATOR
JOHN THOMPSON

MEDIUM
ACRYLIC

277

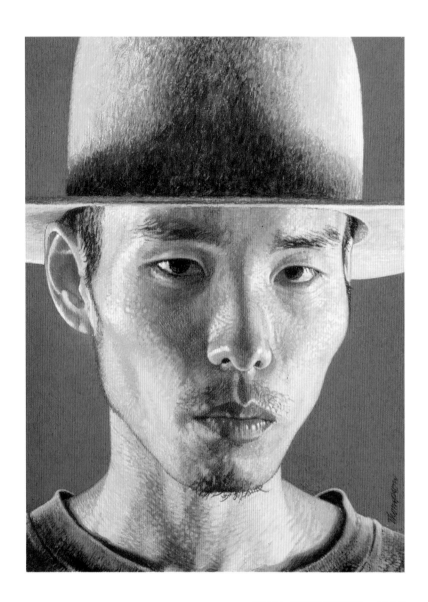

ILLUSTRATOR
TIM O'BRIEN

MEDIUM
OIL ON PANEL

278

JOHN THOMPSON

SELF- PROMOTIONAL
UNPUBLISHED

ILLUSTRATOR
DORTHEA PALMER

MEDIUM
PASTEL

279

ILLUSTRATOR
CHARLY PALMER

MEDIUM
COMPUTER GENERATED

AGENCY
T.P. DESIGN, INC.

CLIENT
ALTERNATIVE PIC

280

SELF– PROMOTIONAL
UNPUBLISHED

ILLUSTRATOR
TIM O'BRIEN

MEDIUM
OIL ON PANEL

281

ILLUSTRATOR
JOE ALCALA

282

SELF- PROMOTIONAL
UNPUBLISHED

ILLUSTRATOR
DAVID TILLINGHAST

MEDIUM
ACRYLIC AND GOLD LEAF ON
ILLUSTRATION BOARD

ART DIRECTOR
DAVID TILLINGHAST

CLIENT
DAVID TILLINGHAST

283

ILLUSTRATOR
DAVID TILLINGHAST

MEDIUM
ACRYLIC ON CANVAS

ART DIRECTOR
DAVID TILLINGHAST

CLIENT
GAIL IMSTEPF

284

SELF- PROMOTIONAL
UNPUBLISHED

ILLUSTRATOR
DOUGLAS FRASER

MEDIUM
DIGITAL

285

ILLUSTRATOR
HALSTEAD HANNAH

MEDIUM
ACRYLIC, OIL, PRISMACOLOR,
AIRBRUSH

286

SELF– PROMOTIONAL
UNPUBLISHED

ILLUSTRATOR
RICK FARRELL

MEDIUM
OIL

287

ILLUSTRATOR
HERMAN WEEB

CLIENT
OBLIQUE COMMUNICATIONS

288

SELF- PROMOTIONAL
UNPUBLISHED

ILLUSTRATOR
JEFFREY HITCH

MEDIUM
ACRYLIC

289

ILLUSTRATOR
CHUCK LEAL

290

SELF- PROMOTIONAL
UNPUBLISHED

ILLUSTRATOR
ROBERT JEW

MEDIUM
ACRYLIC ON WOOD

291

ILLUSTRATOR
NICK GALIFIANAKIS

MEDIUM
WATER COLOR

ART DIRECTOR
SAM WARD

CLIENT
NICK GALIFIANAKIS

292

**SELF- PROMOTIONAL
UNPUBLISHED**

ILLUSTRATOR
JOHN ENGLISH

MEDIUM
OIL ON CANVAS

ART DIRECTOR
BETH JOHNSON

ART DIRECTOR
FRIEND & JOHNSON ARTIST'S REP

293

ILLUSTRATOR
JOHN ENGLISH

MEDIUM
OIL ON CANVAS

ART DIRECTOR
JOHN ENGLISH

294

ILLUSTRATOR
JOHN ENGLISH

MEDIUM
OIL ON CANVAS

ART DIRECTOR
JOHN ENGLISH

295

ILLUSTRATOR
JOHN ENGLISH

MEDIUM
OIL ON CANVAS

ART DIRECTOR
BETH JOHNSON

CLIENT
FRIEND & JOHNSON ARTIST'S REP

296

SELF- PROMOTIONAL
UNPUBLISHED

ILLUSTRATOR
DOUGLAS TALALLA

MEDIUM
ACRYLIC

299

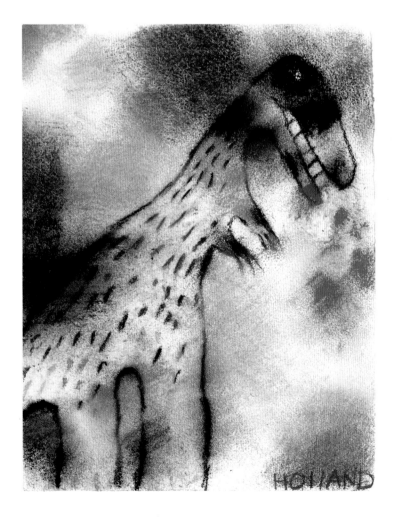

ILLUSTRATOR
BRAD HOLLAND

MEDIUM
PASTEL ON HANDMADE PAPER

ART DIRECTOR
D.K. HOLLAND

AGENCY
PUSHPIN STUDIO

CLIENT
ILLUSTRATION AMERICA

300

SELF– PROMOTIONAL
UNPUBLISHED

ILLUSTRATOR
GREGORY MILLER

MEDIUM
WATER COLOR

303

ILLUSTRATOR
STEVE ATKINSON

MEDIUM
AIRBRUSH, DYES

304

**SELF- PROMOTIONAL
UNPUBLISHED**

ILLUSTRATOR
CATHLEEN TOELKE

CLIENT
SERBIN COMMUNICATIONS

305

ILLUSTRATOR
JOHN ROWE

MEDIUM
OIL

306

SELF– PROMOTIONAL
UNPUBLISHED

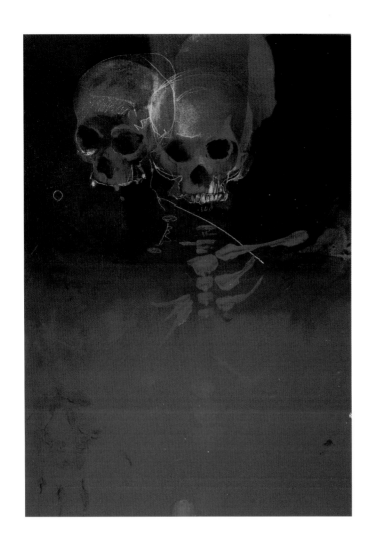

ILLUSTRATOR
JOHN ROWE

MEDIUM
MIXED MEDIA

307

ILLUSTRATOR
BILL MAYER

308

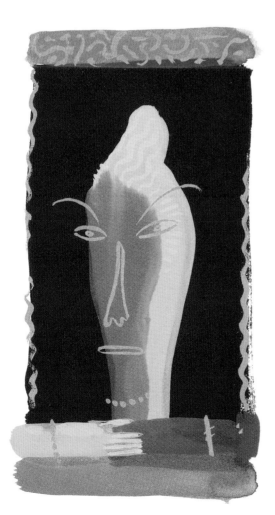

**SELF– PROMOTIONAL
UNPUBLISHED**

ILLUSTRATOR
BILL MAYER

309

ILLUSTRATOR
ROB SAUBER

MEDIUM
WATER COLOR

310

STUDENT

GOLD MEDAL

ROBERT GRODT

SILVER MEDAL

REGAN SCHUYLAR

BRONZE MEDAL

MICHAEL RYAN

♥

[STUDENT SILVER MEDAL]

ILLUSTRATOR
REGAN SCHUYLAR

MEDIUM
ALKYD, OIL

312

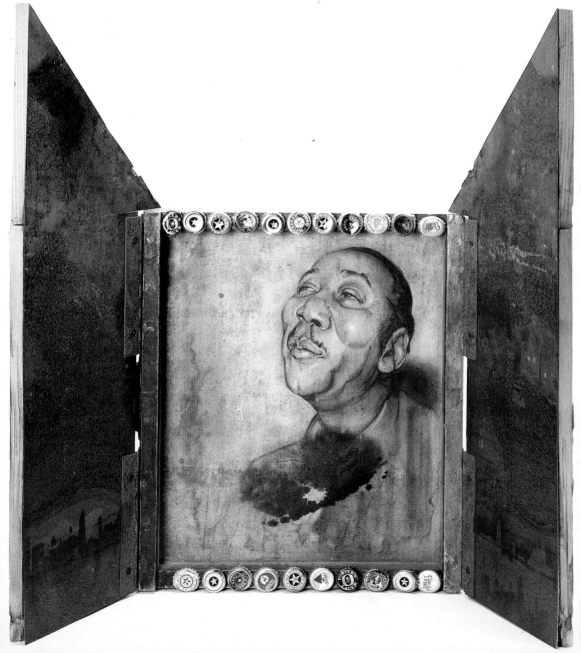

[STUDENT HONORABLE MENTION]

ILLUSTRATOR
DAVID CHEN

MEDIUM
MIXED MEDIA

314

[STUDENT HONORABLE MENTION]

ILLUSTRATOR
DAVID CHEN

MEDIUM
MIXED MEDIA

315

ILLUSTRATOR
ALFREDO MERCADO

MEDIUM
MIXED MEDIA

316

ILLUSTRATOR
JOHN MARTIN

MEDIUM
ACRYLIC, COLORED PENCIL

317

ILLUSTRATOR
JENNIFER KOSTECKI

MEDIUM
MIXED MEDIA

318

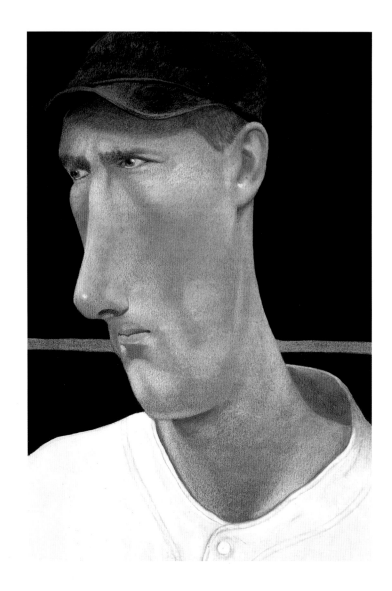

ILLUSTRATOR
STEVE SIEGRIST

319

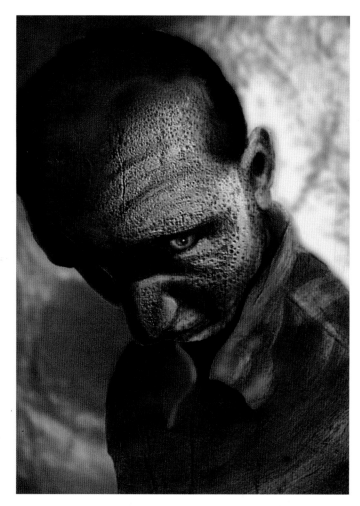

ILLUSTRATOR
P J LOUGHRAN

MEDIUM
ACRYLIC PAINT,
INDIA INK OVERLAY

320

ILLUSTRATOR
ANDY CLARK

321

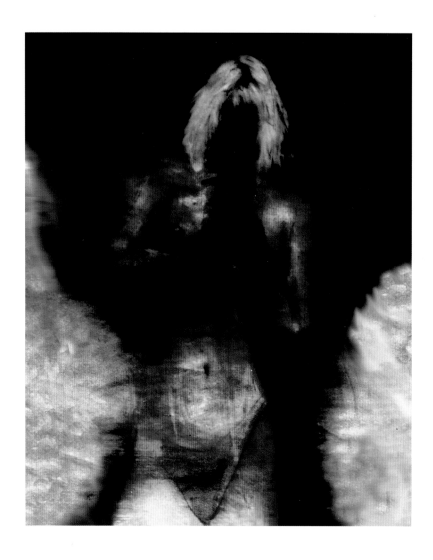

ILLUSTRATOR
TERRY COOLIDGE

MEDIUM
CHARCOAL, PASTEL

324

ILLUSTRATOR
PATRICK KOCHAKJI

325

ILLUSTRATOR
TAKASHI MORISHIMA

MEDIUM
MIXED MEDIA

328

ILLUSTRATOR
RICHARD EWING

MEDIUM
ACRYLIC

329

SPONSORS

ARCHIVE

WWW

TYPE
GRAPHIC DESIGN

PRINTING
LARGE
FORMAT

CLIENT SERVICES

DIGITAL MEDIA IMAGING

DIGITAL RETOUCHING

DIGITAL PHOTOGRAPHY

DIGITAL Pre-Press

DIGITAL PRINTING

DIGITAL COMMUNCATIONS

IMAGE CONSULT

Where
Your
Image
Becomes
Reality

GRAFICO INC.
15320 CORNET AVENUE
SANTA FE SPRINGS, CA 90670
562 921 6731   714 521 0620
FAX 562 921 7038
WWW.GRAFICO.COM

DIGITAL MEDIA IMAGING ™

We'Re WaY AheaD oF YoU!

At **Pacific Rim International Printing**, your corrections can be made yesterday even though we just got the changes this morning. Confusing? Not to us. Our Hong Kong facilities are a day ahead of you — giving us a maximum time advantage.

We also save you money. Pacific Rim International offers the highest **quality** at the **best prices**. Our high level of **expertise** and **personal service** have given us a leading edge in high color, sheetfed production of case and perfect bound books, catalogs, brochures, calendars, greeting cards, posters, **and more!**

We Offer You:

- Full Scale Electronic Prepress and Print Production
- Special Die Cutting, Embossing and Foiling Capabilities
- Digital Scanning and Retouching
- International Distribution
- Design Services & Networking

Our clients depend on us. And **we deliver!** It's no wonder they keep coming back year after year.

Pacific Rim International Printing
Ahead of the rest...here to stay!

Call 1-800-95-COLOR or fax 310 207-2566 today!
11726 San Vicente Blvd., Suite 280, Los Angeles, CA 90049

THE ILLUSTRATION ACADEMY

ONE-WEEK SESSION
May 20 - May 25

FIRST-FOUR-WEEK SESSION
May 25 - June 20

SECOND FOUR-WEEK SESSION
June 22 - July 18

FOR INFORMATION WRITE TO:
The Illustration Academy
5844 Fontana Drive
Fairway, KS 66205

OR CALL:
913-789-8878

MARK ENGLISH
JOHN COLLIER
JOHN ENGLISH
BART FORBES
GARY KELLEY
ANITA KUNZ
SKIP LIEPKE
FRED OTNES
C.F. PAYNE
GREG SPALENKA
JACK UNRUH
BRENT WATKINSON

THE ILLUSTRATION ACADEMY offers art students and professionals the opportunity to study with some of the most successful and exciting illustrators working today. See the art and talk to the artist who set the pace in the field. Improve your work, your work habits, and your portfolios.

THE ILLUSTRATION ACADEMY offers a one-week, and two four-week intensive workshops to be held in the summer of 1997 at William Jewell College in Liberty, Missouri. Room and board are available; up to twelve hours of college credit offered through William Jewell College.

SOCIETY OF ILLUSTRATORS OF LOS ANGELES

MEMBERSHIP AND ILLUSTRATION WEST INFORMATION

Nationwide in scope, The Society of Illustrators of Los Angeles is a not-for-profit organization consisting of professional and student illustrators dedicated to education and social interaction between illustrators and the community at large. There are frequent educational seminars, programs and workshops open to the public, where issues of importance are presented to illustrators and people working in the graphic arts fields. Illustration West, now in it's 35th consecutive year, is potentially the largest juried exhibition of illustration work west of New York, with over 300 original works exhibited. SILA has a student scholarship program, along with other community service projects such as an Air Force Art program, Sheriff's Documentary Art program, and The Children's Hospital program. Membership is open to all professional illustrators, full-time illustration students, or those allied to the field.

Please write to the address below for further information on membership in our organization or to order additional copies of this annual.

THE SOCIETY OF ILLUSTRATORS OF LOS ANGELES
116 The Plaza Pasadena
Pasadena, CA. 91101
818.551.1760
http://www.Grafico.com/Grafico/sila/SilaHome.html

Society of Illustrators of Los Angeles

Illustration by Robert Rodriguez